SAN JUAN ISLAND LIBRARY DISTRICT

3 3186 00123 3921

P9-DMK-451

SAN JUAN ISLAND LIBRARY
1010 GUARD STREET
FRIDAY HARBOR, WA 98250

11 '03
DEMCO

Agnès's
Final Afternoon

ALSO BY FRANÇOIS RICARD

L'Incroyable Odyssée, novella (1981)
La Littérature contre elle-même, essays (1985)
The Lyric Generation, essay (1992)
Gabrielle Roy: A Life, biography (1996)

Agnès's Final Afternoon

AN ESSAY ON THE WORK OF MILAN KUNDERA

François Ricard

Translated from the French by
Aaron Asher

HarperCollins*Publishers*

AGNÈS'S FINAL AFTERNOON. Copyright © 2003 by François Ricard. Translation copyright © 2003 by Aaron Asher. All rights reserved. Printed in the United States of America. No part of this book may be used or reproduced in any manner whatsoever without written permission except in the case of brief quotations embodied in critical articles and reviews. For information, address HarperCollins Publishers Inc., 10 East 53rd Street, New York, NY 10022.

HarperCollins books may be purchased for educational, business, or sales promotional use. For information, please write: Special Markets Department, HarperCollins Publishers Inc., 10 East 53rd Street, New York, NY 10022.

First published in France in 2003 as *Le dernier après-midi d'Agnès* by Editions Gallimard.

FIRST EDITION

Designed by Kimba Baker-Feketé

Printed on acid-free paper

Library of Congress Cataloging-in-Publication Data

Ricard, François.
  [Le dernier après-midi d'Agnès. English]
    Agnès's final afternoon : an essay on the work of Milan Kundera / François Ricard ; translated from the French by Aaron Asher.—1st ed.
      p.   cm.
  Includes bibliographical references.
  ISBN 0-06-000564-5
    1. Kundera, Milan—Criticism and interpretation.
  I. Asher, Aaron. II. Title.

PG5039.21.U6Z86713 2003
891.8'685409—dc21   2002191932

03 04 05 06 07 ❖/RRD   10 9 8 7 6 5 4 3 2 1

SAN JUAN ISLAND LIBRARY
1010 GUARD STREET
FRIDAY HARBOR, WA 98250

Contents

Agnès's
Final Afternoon

Prologue

*Perhaps admiration is not delight but rather a kind of attention.
What one admires in reflecting on a work of art is an inexplicable
interest that excludes any plan; it is a sufficiency of the moment
itself and lacks desire. It is like a pedestrian on a Paris bridge stopping to contemplate. . . .*

ALAIN*

An appropriate means of approaching Milan Kundera's
work to date is to put ourselves mentally and morally
into Agnès's situation at the beginning of Part Five of
the novel *Immortality*, when, before continuing on the
road to Paris, she decides to spend another afternoon in
Switzerland, amid the mountains that for her are an
area of silence and memory. This episode, which in a
way will "cause" Agnès's death, can be pondered both
as a great lesson in reading and literary criticism and as
an illustration par excellence of the Kunderian concept
and practice of the art of the novel.

What first strikes us is the entirely unmotivated,
even illogical, nature of Agnès's decision and of her
behavior under the circumstances. We know that "she

*Alain, *Propos de littérature* (Paris, 1969), p. 60.

[doesn't] like to drive at night" and thus plans to arrive in Paris at a sensible hour. And that it is a long drive. Instead of taking the wheel and forging ahead toward her destination, she lingers, disregards her initial intention, and loses precious time. What's going on, why isn't she leaving? Why does she let herself be distracted by what is only scenery, a chance detail, a small contingency that her plan (to get home before nightfall) ought to preclude her from paying attention to at this moment? Why this sudden immobility that, against all reason, defers action and puts her journey (her life) in jeopardy? The novel gives only this answer:

> Like a lover who has failed to say everything that is
> in his heart, the surrounding landscape stopped her
> from leaving. She got out of the car. There were
> mountains all around her. . . .

In the first and last of these three sentences, Agnès is not the subject but the object of the action, the "victim," the prisoner. She doesn't leave because her will has been superseded by a stronger one, mysteriously coming from the landscape, ordering her to stay. And yet we know very well that it would be easy for her to ignore that order and escape these pleasant surroundings; it is what nearly all of us do; it is what her motorcyclist husband, Paul, whom no landscape ever stops from going on his way, does. To keep to her schedule Agnès need only turn on the ignition and zoom off directly to Paris. But there is that second sentence, the most important because it will trigger the rest of the story: "She got out of the car." This time it is Agnès who acts, or chooses *not* to act, not to turn the key, to stay where she is and to delay herself. It is she, in other words, who decides to obey the landscape's command, to listen to the voice that wants to speak to her, to let herself be surrounded, possessed, dominated by the desire of that "lover" to whom she is offering her person and her freedom. Like a slave, like that lover's lover, she chooses to give herself entirely to the mountains.

And from then on, for the rest of the afternoon, the mountains will hold her in their grip. They will govern her every step, fill her senses and her thoughts, draw her irresistibly outside herself, outside the headlong and practical tempo of her life so as to bring her into another tempo, their own tempo, a tempo of slowness and contemplation that Agnès no longer controls, that no longer "serves" her, that, literally, turns her away from the route she has marked, but that—at the same time, and without her prior knowledge—will lead her toward the darkest and most luminous secret.

In short, Agnès becomes a reader of the mountains. For reading, what's known as reading, always begins with that coming to a halt, that consent of the mind and the imagination to their abdication, even their servitude—that is, to the overturning of the power we usually claim over our ideas, our projects, our needs, our very existence. The true reader (if such still exist) is always that "gentle reader" addressed in the Prologue to *Don Quixote*, a reader who has left behind his activities and his aims, who has interrupted his journey and who—"prevented from leaving" by the beauty before his eyes—delays himself and everything he had intended and planned. Opening a book, letting oneself be "surrounded" by a book, getting oneself in the position of being oneself "read" by a book—at least if the book is a novel—initially requires one to "get out of the car"; that is, to withdraw not only from the familiar reality that surrounds us, as the convention of fiction stipulates, but also, and more fundamentally still, withdraw from our personal history, from our social, political, emotional allegiances, from our "researches" and our theories—from our identity itself, if that's possible. Without such abdication, such initial "distraction," no reading can take place, no discovery or wonder, but merely the reiteration of what we know, desire, and are already. Just as the Agnès who yields to the mountains is no longer the Agnès who a moment before was in a hurry to zoom off to Paris, the reading "I" is always a different person from the everyday "I."

A different person and, inevitably, a kind of traitor. What is Agnès actually doing when she removes the ignition key so as to respond to the landscape's call? She is cutting the thread of her present life, she is putting a parenthesis into the sequence of actions and thoughts that allow her to conduct her existence; she is dissociating from herself and betraying herself. In a way she is also betraying her family awaiting her in Paris. This treason rests entirely on the simple fact of stopping, of no longer advancing along the planned route, and like an exhausted runner giving up, *sidestepping*, which by relieving him of all haste robs him of both victory and defeat. With regard to the world as with regard to herself and her destiny, Agnès finds herself suddenly out of the game, in the position of a laggard, an exile, a missing person. She is no longer there; the car is empty and as if dead in the hotel parking lot; all around, there is only the calm and indecipherable plenitude of the mountains. Now anything can happen.

I would like this essay on Kundera's oeuvre to resemble Agnès's final afternoon. To be immersed in the same climate, to keep to the same movement, thus to proceed from the same absorption with the oeuvre before us and, therefore, with the same disregard for the rules and ambitions of scholarly criticism, which we leave behind in Agnès's suitcase, tossed casually on the backseat of her car. Perhaps this is not a study or even a book of literary criticism but rather a *meditation*, which is probably what the misunderstood art of the essay ought to be called. No theory of the novel or political doctrine or philosophy is to be found here, merely the account of an aesthetic experience, of endless admiration and exploration of an oeuvre that is one of the most perfect and invaluable of our time. That is why my reading hopes primarily to be—if the adjective has not yet been devalued—an *internal* reading: a reading that works itself out within the very core of the oeuvre, considering that oeuvre not as its "subject" but as its "place," meaning that the mind that is reading it will no longer be separated from it.

As for my method, I will have only the one taught by Agnès herself, who for me will be, like Lucie for the young Ludvik of *The Joke*, an "usherette," a guide, my Beatrice. Confronting Kundera's writings, I will try not only to maintain a state of mind like the one impelling Agnès on that afternoon amid the mountains but also, as nearly as possible, to imitate her actions, follow in her footsteps, stay constantly at her side, in her shadow, so that her way of approaching the landscape, exploring it, being transformed by it, becomes mine as well.

Sidestepping

When she was little, her father taught her to play chess. She was *fascinated by one move, technically called castling: . . . the enemy concentrates all his effort on attacking the king, and the king suddenly disappears before his eyes; he moves away. All her life she dreamed about that move, and the more exhausted she felt, the more she dreamed it.*

MILAN KUNDERA

Before we turn, along with her, toward the spectacle of the mountains, let's linger a little longer over that very first moment, when Agnès leaves her car and gazes at the landscape. A metaphor for reading and a lesson in criticism, this gesture has all the more force and accuracy in that we can also see it as a more generic metaphor: that of the Kunderian novel itself, or at least one of its essential characteristics.

The Novel of Fighting

To understand this characteristic, one might look to Hegel's classic definition of modern fiction: "As individuals with their subjective ends of love, honour, and ambition, or with their ideals of world-reform, [the heroes of modern fiction] stand opposed to [the] substantial order and the prose of actuality which puts difficulties in their way on all sides. Therefore, in this opposition, subjective wishes and demands are screwed up to immeasurable heights; for each man finds before him an enchanted and quite alien world he must fight because it obstructs him and its inflexible firmness does not give way to his passions. . . . Now the thing is to breach this order of things, to change the world, to improve it, or at least in spite of it to carve out of it a heaven upon earth." The engine of the novelistic imagination would thus be conflict or, rather, the confrontation "between the poetry of the heart and the opposing prose of circumstances";* that is, between the desire of the individual thirsting for meaning and fulfillment and the degraded world into which he has been cast, a conflict summarized by Georg Lukács in a well-known phrase: "The novel is

*G. W. F. Hegel, *Aesthetics*, trans. T. M. Knox (London, 1975), vol. 1, pp. 592–93; vol. 2, p. 1092.

the epic of a world that has been abandoned by God."*
"Epic," meaning war, struggle, and the relationship,
both problematic and polemical, between a hero and
the reality facing him.

Still according to Hegel's definition, such confrontation can lead only to the elimination of one of the two
antagonists: either the hero relinquishes his aspirations
and resigns himself to reality as it is, or he turns away
from reality and forever shuts himself off into his
desires. In other words, either he discovers the prose of
the world and forges into it (Rastignac), or he sticks to
his poetry and no longer has a place in the world
(Werther). But in both instances the end of the conflict
means the end of the novel. Above all else, the novel is
the story of the exertions or setbacks of the hero, that
"modern knight" (says Hegel) and his tribulations,
whether they lead him ultimately to triumph or failure,
will appear as so many milestones in the pursuit of that
constant fighting—now apprenticeship, now rebellion—
that is his novelistic destiny.

Bound to this model of the "novel of fighting" are
such elements of novelistic form as suspense, sudden
turns, dramatic progression, temporal linearity, and so
on. Since it has older roots (*Don Quixote, Robinson Cru-*

*Georg Lukács, *The Theory of the Novel*, trans. Anna Bostock (Cam-
bridge, Mass., 1971), p. 88.

soe) and takes shape in exemplary fashion in the so-called *Bildungsroman* or the adventure novel, and later on in the thriller, we might say that it is globally valid (with few exceptions) for all of what Kundera, in *Testaments Betrayed*, calls the "second half" of the novel's history—that is, the nineteenth century and even beyond. The typical novel in the modern imagination, a bit like the tale in the folkloric imagination, is above all the story of the transformation (positive or negative) of an individual or of a world; its logic and organization are those of a quest (or conquest or inquest)—the enactment of a desire (for glory, love, wealth, happiness, truth); and its central character, no matter whether he triumphs or is crushed, is always in some way, "a hero," a person on the move, someone doing battle. In this respect Zola is not much different from Hugo or Dumas, or Malraux from Melville or Balzac, or even Proust from Stendhal and Dostoevsky. That is probably the main way in which the novel is so profoundly in harmony with the modern sensibility, for which history and existence are inconceivable apart from movement, from the march forward, and from fighting.

The power—and at once the terrible weight—of this model may appear most clearly in Kafka's work, which reveals it even as it perverts and thus exhausts it. Indeed, in the pre-Kafka novel, the hero's fight was based on a fundamentally "optimistic" vision of the world in which he had to live and battle. A world without gods, deprived of transcendental necessity and fallen into instability, was a world that seemed to be malleable, perfectible material, and thus—in principle—open to the transforming (or destructive) actions of the hero, whose victory, however arduous and uncertain it seemed, stood on the horizon of the *possible* and from there exercised an appeal that justified, supported, and ceaselessly resumed the battle. Rastignac, Julien Sorel, Emma Bovary, Anna Karenina, even Proust's Marcel in *À la recherche du temps perdu,* can at least think that their aspirations have some chance of being fulfilled and that the world might yield to their desire. Their fight thus has a meaning, and even if they lose, they can expect to pull through with what the military of old called an honorable defeat.

Now, in Kafka this kind of assurance, which used to surround the heroes of novels, is no longer in practice. Represented by the invisible tribunal that has convicted Josef K. or by the equally invisible authorities who forbid the surveyor's access to the castle, the horizon here is permanently blocked, and the world that surrounds and faces the character has become completely impenetrable. Its victory, or its immutability, meaning the crushing of the hero, is assured from the start and for all eternity;

no logic can prevail against its blind and unwarranted power, no attack can shake it; it is there, silent and forever invulnerable. Of this opaque and heavy world we can no longer even say that it constitutes an obstacle to be overcome or an enemy the individual and his desire must confront. Its silence and immobility put it beyond reach of any attack, it is the *absolute beyond*, the thing we can no longer address, no longer know or love or hate, the thing we can no longer rise up against or even protest, for there is no longer either language or anything else in common between it and oneself, between that absence and the hero's actions and desire.

Under such conditions it's obvious—it should be obvious—that the "epic" duel between the individual and reality cannot take place. The adversaries are no longer equal, and the hero's every act inevitably turns against him, only hastening and confirming his ruin. And yet the hero does act: Josef K. tries to defend himself and prove his innocence; the surveyor goes right on with his efforts, relentlessly, persistent still, at the foot of the inaccessible castle, behaving like Rastignac, who at least had Paris at his feet. What is tragic—and which is also the whole joke—in Kafka comes from this incongruity: just as Gregor Samsa, in "The Metamorphosis," goes on, despite his new condition, thinking and planning like a traveling salesman and a devoted son, and just as the characters in *The Trial* and *The Castle*, caught in a universe where the powers are far too unequal for the battle to have any meaning and where no "adventure" can thus any longer arise, continue—instinctively, as if it were the only thing they *can* do—to battle and act as "heroes." Confronted by a reality that has ceased to be alterable and that is therefore no longer even hostile but just radically *other*, their only recourse is the old model, the old reflex inherited from romanticism: that of confrontation and quest.

Few contemporary novelists have taken note of the exhaustion of the Hegelian novelistic model (and of the historical and metaphysical consciousness that underlie it) as precisely and perceptively as the author of *The Joke* and *Immortality*. What to do from then on, when all fighting is futile? What remains for the surveyor or for Josef K. after the death of the illusion into which their behavior as heroes locked them? What does the novel become when the epic model is no longer tenable and the world has become crazy? It is primarily by the answer it attempts to bring to these questions, or in any case the way in which it asks them, that Kundera's oeuvre is a child of Kafka's, and for that reason, one of the most "topical" we can read.

Of this answer the scene in which Agnès decides against resuming her drive to Paris and stays in the mountains offers an illustration. What happens in that moment? Simply this: a person suddenly comes to a standstill. He discards his weapons, he leaves the bat-tlefield. He becomes that unexpected, paradoxical, specifically Kunderian hero—he who, repudiating his position as hero, has *abandoned the fight*.

With this action (or *inaction*) Agnès entirely defines herself; it is the moment when she coincides most exactly with herself. From the beginning of the novel, actually, she has been presented as a character who "felt no solidarity with mankind," because of "the strong, peculiar feeling that was coming over her more and more often":

> She had nothing in common with those two-legged creatures with a head on their shoulders and a mouth in their face. There was a time when she was inter-ested in their politics, their science, their inventions, when she considered herself a small part of their great adventure, until one day the feeling was born in her that she did not belong among them. . . . She was no longer able to torment herself with thoughts of their wars nor to enjoy their celebrations, because she was filled with the conviction that none of it was her concern.

Until her trip to Switzerland, that feeling had remained more or less buried, secret, relegated to the unacknowledgable: it was a "strange feeling" that "she resisted . . . she knew that it was absurd as well as amoral," and that consequently did not completely govern her life but nonetheless did haunt her, and—in her relations with her husband, Paul; her sister, Laura; or her daughter, Brigitte; as well as in her work and in her errands amid the Paris throngs—kept growing clearer, more pervasive in her, despite her resistance. But she tried to act as if that feeling did not exist, or to give in to it as little as possible, continuing to live as if there were still some connection between her and the world, even if only that of aversion. A sprig of forget-me-not in hand, she was prepared to make a public display of the rebellion the city's ugliness and noise inspired in her; to thrash a passerby who jostled her; to wish death on the rider of a too-noisy motorcycle; even, as she ends up doing, to break Laura's sunglasses; in short, to fight or at least to defend herself against external aggressions and to behave so that somehow her own values triumph.

This whole area of desire and "fighting" (the title and theme of the novel's Part Three) Agnès leaves behind her when she gets out of her car and turns toward the mountains, thus giving in to, finally giving in to, the feeling, previously "absurd and amoral," now immensely relaxing, of her nonbelonging. It is the end of confrontation, of the idea of "playing a small part in [some] great adventure." All she seeks from now on is not to be among "those creatures" anymore, to be on her own somewhere else, where their clamor and agitation will no longer reach her. She is not their enemy, she does not hound them with her hatred, she has no wish to eliminate or vanquish them, she has simply ceased "to belong among them." She has ceased, in other words, not only to belong to their universe and believe in their adventure but also to believe in her own adventure and in the necessity of fighting for the achievement of projects and desires she no longer cares about. She who was already "on the other side of love," in her sister's accusation, is now beyond all fighting as well. Presaged by her earlier "strange feeling," her desertion, her entry into "noncombatant" territory is now complete.

The Novel of Exile

Agnès's sidestepping is by no means unique in Kundera's oeuvre. In one form or another it is the fact for all the "principal" characters we meet there, the characters whose presence constitutes, in all the novels and stories, both the most active and most solid center of meaning. To recall, let's list them: Klara's lover, Dr. Havel, and Eduard in *Laughable Loves*; Ludvik in *The Joke*; "the man in his forties" in *Life Is Elsewhere*; Jakub in *Farewell Waltz*; Tamina (and Jan) in *The Book of Laughter and Forgetting*; Tomas and Sabina in *The Unbearable Lightness of Being*; the Chevalier and Madame de T. in *Slowness*; Chantal in *Identity*; Josef in *Ignorance*. Although their status in the narrative might vary—now a protagonist, now a secondary or even transitory figure—in their respective books each occupies a central *thematic* position: from them emanates the distinctive light that illuminates and colors all the rest; it is they whose gaze, so to speak, is the very gaze of the novel itself. In the existence of each of them we meet again, in various forms and tonalities, the same anti-Hegelian novelistic model, or the same antimodel: that of the deserter, the person who chooses not to confront the world anymore, to abandon the fight, to disappear. That disappearance, to which we'll have to return, can be achieved in many ways. But each time it lays out the same motifs of bifurcation, of "disengagement," of a progressive or sudden splitting by which consciousness loses its interest in what had hitherto held sway over it, withdraws the credit it had granted from the values, goals, and desires that had hitherto been guiding it, and takes off along a crossroad.

There, at once revealed and ceaselessly questioned by the existence of these "principal" characters, lies what we can consider the very spirit of the Kunderian novel: the original outlook, the founding psychological and aesthetic attitude that powers the novelistic imagination and thereafter keeps governing and nourishing its developments. That outlook always consists, as in Agnès's case, of a form of disaffection, of radical dissociation from the world and from oneself, from the self in the world; it is an emigration, an exile.

The mental attitude discussed here strongly resembles the "conversion" of the hero described by René Girard at the conclusion of his *Mensonge romantique et vérité romanesque*. The "renunciation of metaphysical desire" with which all the great novels end is pretty much the same thing as Agnès's gesture, in that it too involves a distancing whereby the hero finally deserts a world entirely given over to superficiality, imitation, and fighting. But Girard's analyses are inspired mainly by nineteenth-century works (Stendhal, Flaubert, Dostoevsky, Proust, with a retrospective detour to *Don Quixote*), by what I've called the "Hegelian" type of novel, built on relentless fighting between the individual and the world. That is probably why, between the Girardian vision of the hero's conversion and the Kunderian experience of exile as lived by Agnès and the other characters I've named, there exist at least two important differences.

The first concerns the *direction* of the hero's "departure." In Girard's perspective the conversion is

in fact an ascent: The character "escapes *upward*"*
from the world's disorders and torments. So it is, for
example, with the "genuine passion [that] succeeds
[the] madness [of desire] among the best of Stendhal's
heroes": "[It] merges," Girard writes, "with the seren-
ity of the *summits* these heroes reach in supreme
moments. . . . In the Farnese Tower, Fabrice and Clélia
experience a happy repose *above* the desires and the
superficiality that still threaten but never hurt them."
Here to free oneself is to rise; it is, in Baudelaire's
words, finally to find, "far from morbid miasmas," the
"upper air" where the "bright fire" of reconciliation
shines. The light and peacefulness this freedom brings
have something of the celestial, and that is why Girard,
at the conclusion of his work, can give it, if not the
content, at least the color of a religious experience—
that is to say, of a kind of redemption verging on tran-
scendence.

There is none of this in the Kunderian character's
desertion. Agnès's final afternoon is of course set in the
altitude and pure air of the mountains. But the interior
experience of which it is the outcome, and which
equally marks the existence of the other "principal"
Kundera characters, is not so much the discovery of a

---

*All the citations in this paragraph come from René Girard, *Mensonge
romantique et vérité romanesque* (Paris, 1978), pp. 35–36 (italics mine).

tranquil summit overlooking the plain where the noise and fury of the world are raging, but rather of a periphery, of a remote, abandoned place, a kind of desert island where it's not a matter of seeing or of triumphing over someone or something, but rather of no longer being seen, of withdrawing, of escaping all adversaries. The movement that leads to this place is thus not vertical but lateral; like a chess king whom the rook protects by "moving out," by castling, this is not a step beyond but a sidestep, not a rise but a defection. Or else, if there is a shift on the vertical axis, it is downward, and the liberation of the hero—as can be seen particularly (but not only) in *The Joke*—then amounts to his *fall*. But in either case the Kunderian "conversion" always remains basically "atheistic." It is never a truth winning out over a lie; what happens is more like the opposite: abandonment of the desire for truth, and the awareness, both sad and amused, resigned and compassionate, of the ubiquity of lying, an awareness that is surely the most accurate definition of *unbelief*. The character is drawn not to surpass or dominate the world, or to surpass or dominate himself, but to leave, to expel himself both from the world and from his own fate; this gives him not redemption but the sensual pleasure of laughter and forgetting. It is not an apotheosis; it is, as I've said, an exile.

The other feature through which Kundera's novels largely elude Girard's analysis is that the sudden disaffection that marks the existence of their "principal" characters—or at least most of them—occurs neither only nor necessarily at the end of their story, as Girard says is the case with the romantic heroes he studies. The "happy repose" of Fabrice and Clélia, the "sublime lucidity" Dostoevsky's characters achieve, the "disillusion" of Don Quixote, the "time regained" of Proust's narrator—all these events are conclusions: they not only rescue the hero *in extremis* and bring him a kind of victory but also represent the negation or overcoming of everything he has been and experienced up until then. That is why they can only take place at the very end of the story—most often with the character's dying and death—without which the novel literally cannot take place, the novel that all along, in conformity with that Hegelian model, is nothing but a battlefield traveled by tumult and violence, entirely permeated by the war that individuals, beginning with the hero, wage on the world and one another. We can summarize this outline as follows: the hero goes through the world like a blind man, then leaves it just when he regains his sight; his conversion—his healing—thus ends the novel.

One of the ventures of the Kunderian oeuvre is radically to modify this outline by no longer making dis-

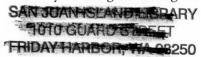
SAN JUAN ISLAND LIBRARY
1010 GUARD STREET
FRIDAY HARBOR, WA 98250

enchantment the outcome or the "conclusion" of the hero's existence but rather the moral and aesthetic climate in which the entire life is steeped. Not a time-bound event, however lofty, but a state or inclination functioning throughout the whole novel. When Agnès deserts her car and turns toward the mountains, her death is surely imminent, *but the end of the novel is not*, and the same Agnès reappears in Part Six. Moreover, the "strange feeling" of nonbelonging, which she has always associated with the example and memory of her father, is already old for her; so that this nonbelonging really forms the basis—the *"Grund"*—of her being and of her life. In this way Agnès is primarily a post-Hegelian or post-Romantic heroine par excellence: unlike Fabrice or Julien Sorel, unlike the possessed Dostoevsky characters, unlike Swann or Marcel, at no moment of her existence does she desire to enter the world; on the contrary she seeks only one thing: to leave it. The "awakening" that strikes the romantic hero at the end of his journey in her case takes the form of a question that is always with her:

> How to live in a world with which you disagree? How to live with people when you share neither their suffering nor their joys? When you know that you don't belong among them?

Here as elsewhere in Kundera everything thus happens as if the person's liberation or emigration *had already taken place* and as if the entire novel sprang from it, continued and deepened it by patiently unfolding its consequences, and reiterated it ceaselessly.

René Girard, too, notes, apropos the romantic hero's final conversion, that it retrospectively affects the whole novel, and that the conclusion thus paradoxically becomes the source of the gaze that makes its possessor "*capable of writing the novel.*" But this "new and more detached vision," suddenly arising afterward, can no longer belong to the character; it is henceforth "the vision of the author himself," who so to speak inherits it with the skin of his hero, who can only be the subject or the target, never the origin. Now, in Kundera that gaze arises and is exercised in the very interior of the novel, from the start and throughout its entire course. To put it in Girard's terms, it is as if the novel, from beginning to end, takes place *after* its conclusion, *beyond* the hero's death (which by the way is indeed the case with the narrative structure of certain parts of *Immortality* and *The Unbearable Lightness of Being*).

It is in this sense, notably, that we can read Kundera's oeuvre as the exploration of a devastated or abandoned world, of the world as it ceaselessly appears to the exiled consciousness. Just as the stories gathered in the *Decameron* are illuminated throughout by the flight from Florence of Pampinea's small group, or those in *Jacques the Fatalist* by the endless wanderings of two companions, so the Kunderian novel originates and feeds on the experience and vision of someone who is endlessly in the process of moving off and vanishing— like Agnès that afternoon, when she forgets the time and sidesteps toward the mountains.

A Panorama

My method of approaching Kundera's oeuvre, as I've said, will follow Agnès's actions as closely as possible. That is why it will consist of three stages, which replicate the three successive moments that shape, like a choreography of contemplation, the unfolding of the final afternoon of her life: overview, walk, repose.

The first of these moments, which occurs just after she gets out of her car, is brief, nearly covert: before she enters the landscape, Agnès, following the model of the "Wanderer" in a painting by Hans Thoma, takes in its immensity with a single look.

> There were mountains all around her; those on the left were clear and bright, and the whiteness of the glaciers shimmered above the green contours; the

mountains on the right were wrapped in a yellowish haze that turned them into silhouettes. They were two different kinds of light; two different worlds. She kept turning her head from left to right and from right to left.

What is striking in this initial image, the restraint of the description aside, is the way it establishes the wholeness of the view despite the two "worlds" it contains and whose opposition may represent Agnès's double awareness, split between the fogginess of her existence and the appeal of, or nostalgia for, a distant immobility. Set out from the beginning ("all around her"), that wholeness appears still more strongly at the end, dynamically reconstructed by her observer's panoramic gaze as it falls upon the two "kinds of light" between which the landscape seems to be divided. Plural, changing, situated in the worlds of light and shadow at once, the mountains as viewed from the parking lot of the hotel where Agnès spent the night— that is, from a position at once distant from and contained by them—thus form a vast collection both orderly and diverse: a massif.

So let us do as she does and start by taking a panoramic view of the Kunderian "massif" as it stretches before us, or *around* us. Although not yet complete, it is one of the most extraordinary and majestic in contemporary literature.

An Oeuvre's Borders

A question immediately arises: Where does that massif begin and end? "There are," Kundera writes, "two notions of an 'oeuvre.' Either one considers everything the author has written as his oeuvre . . . or his oeuvre is only what the author considers valid at the moment of taking stock. I have always been a vehement partisan of the second notion."* In fact, in his own stocktaking, as in the editorial decisions he has made for the past twenty years, Kundera's choice is stringent: What qualifies as his "work," what is fully "authentic," is only those of his writings that belong to the art of the novel.

This isn't to say that all the rest—that is, everything he wrote before his first novel or alongside his work as a novelist—poetry, translations, plays, essays, prefaces, interviews, and so on, published in Czechoslovakia, France, and elsewhere during the last four or five decades—that all this "production," as abundant as it is diverse, is necessarily without interest. Far from it. His study of the novelist Vladislav Vancura, published in 1960, retains great topicality in Czech criticism. Likewise, such writings as "Culture et existence nationale,"

---

*From the "Author's Note" in the first Czech edition of *The Joke*, published after the country's liberation from Russian occupation (1990), quoted in Kvetoslav Chvatik, *Le Monde romanesque de Milan Kundera* (Paris, 1995), p. 237.

"The Czech Wager," "Prague, poème qui disparaît," and "The Kidnapped West,"* while they constitute positions taken, and penetrating analyses of the situation in Czechoslovakia, during and after the Prague Spring, are at the same time thoughtful political and cultural essays that reach beyond the local or immediate circumstances that inspired them. But these writings have never been republished in book form, and thus stand apart from what he considers as his true, fully intentional, and sanctioned "oeuvre," which is neither a "writer's" work nor that of an "intellectual," engaged or not, dissident or not, but in the most precise and exacting sense of the term, his work as a *novelist*. And nothing else.

Of course, in our era of "hybridization" such concern for artistic purity seems outmoded, indeed a bit pretentious. We've lost both the meaning of "oeuvre"—that edifice consciously and conscientiously erected by an artist's labor and thought—and the meaning of "novel," of its powers and its autonomy. The wish expressed by Kundera to "censor" his own bibliography by "limiting" his work to his novels (and the two book-length essays and play) is a defense and an illustration of these very

*Milan Kundera, "Culture et existence nationale," *Les Temps modernes* 263 (April 1968); "Prague, poème qui disparaît," *Le Débat* 2 (June 1980); *New York Review of Books*, "The Czech Wager" (January 22, 1981), and "The Tragedy of Central Europe" (April 26, 1984).

powers and of that autonomy. Hence comes the aston-
ishment that is bound to arise among those, the majority,
who have become incapable of understanding that, in
behaving this way, it is not to himself that the author is
paying homage, but to his art; that it is not his own visage he is sculpting but the work that he has deprived of
(or freed from) his visage, and that in the end has, in a
way, replaced his whole life.

Another consequence of this concern for the oeuvre is
the extreme care with which the author has applied himself, throughout the successive editions and translations
of his work, to give them, materially, an even more perfect and *exact* form to correspond as nearly as possible to
the meaning that each of them seeks. And once that form
is attained—or at least approached as closely as possible—he wants to defend it not only against intentional
alterations but also against the kind of entropy that any
publication or translation brings with it. Here again
nothing is more alien to the temper of our era, with its
fondness for "textual genetics," for "the author's disappearance," and for "deconstruction," than this entirely
exacting vision of the literary text and this utterly "bour-
geois" conception of the author's right to monitor the
texts that appear under his name. We should, therefore,
harbor no illusions. Kundera's wishes—like Kafka's and
those of so many others—concerning the definition of his

"oeuvre" or the texts of his books, however clearly he has expressed them, will end up being betrayed.

Let's at least try as this essay is being written to keep faith with those wishes. The massif before us consists, at this time, of a chain of ten novels whose composition spans the years between 1959 and 1999: *Laughable Loves,** The Joke, Life Is Elsewhere, Farewell Waltz, The Book of Laughter and Forgetting, The Unbearable Lightness of Being, Immortality, Slowness, Identity, Ignorance*. These ten books, the backbone of the body of work, are joined by three others that are not novels but clearly belong to the same aesthetic territory: *Jacques and His Master*, a theatrical variation on Diderot's *Jacques the Fatalist* (completed in Prague in 1971); and two essays,

---

*Two questions come up regarding *Laughable Loves*: (1) Is it a novel or a collection of short stories? The first French edition (1970) presented the book as "short stories," but this indication no longer appears in the "new [French] edition revised by the author" (1986), in which the narratives, without receiving the title "parts" (as in the novels), are nonetheless numbered from I to VII. More recently, in the "Author's Note" for the first Czech edition of that book after the country's liberation (dated 1991 and quoted in Chvatik, *Le Monde romanesque de Milan Kundera)*, the novelist tends to consider it a novel, in a distinctive form, to be sure, but one that is not far removed from that of *The Book of Laughter and Forgetting*. In any case, since in Kundera's view "there is no ontological difference between story and novel" (*Testaments Betrayed*, p. 166), which are only "a small and a large form of the same art" in"Préface" to Lakis Proguidis, *La Conquête du roman* [Paris, 1997], p. xiii), it seems more simple and pertinent not to separate *Laughable Loves* from the novels. (2) Is *Laughable Loves* or *The Joke* Kundera's *first* novel? In the "Author's Note" cited by Chvatik, Kundera considers *The Joke*, completed in 1965, his "Opus 1," and *Laughable Loves*, completed in 1968 but not in its final more or less definitive form until the first French edition, his "Opus 2"; however, the first narrative of *Laughable Loves*, "Nobody Will Laugh," was initially published in 1963, before the completion of *The Joke*.

The Art of the Novel (1985) and *Testaments Betrayed* (1992), works of "aesthetic confession"* and deliberation in which the novel is at once the subject and the source.† These two essays, along with the "Introduction to a Variation" that prefaces *Jacques and His Master*, comprise not only the best description to be found of Kundera's work and "method" but also and above all, rank, in contemporary "theoretical" literature, among the most lucid reflections on the novel and its nature, implications, history, and challenges. Once more, the thought expressed is that of a pure novelist who has total confidence in the novel and cultivates it not as a means or as just one genre among many, but as the very condition, necessary and sufficient, of his connection with the world and with existence itself. Widespread among musicians and poets, such "purity"— that is, such belief in the absolute necessity and sovereignty of their art—is much less common among novelists (and their critics), who, more often than not, hesitate to inhabit the novel—not "literature" or "narrative" or "fiction" or "writing" but the *novel*—as their true, unique, and irreplaceable homeland.

---

*The expression is Kundera's, in "À bâtons rompus," *L'Atelier du roman* 4 (May 1995).
†One should probably add to this "canonical" corpus the ten essays and "Notes" published in the appendix to the French edition of Chvatik, *Le Monde romanesque de Milan Kundera*, pp. 223–57, as well as some other pieces and interviews published since under Kundera's copyright notice.

Topography

Like the circle of mountains Agnès contemplates, the landscape created by Kundera's ten novels is divided, at very first glance, between "two different worlds" separated by the languages in which they have been written. The first is that of the Czech novels; it consists of seven titles whose composition stretches over some thirty years. The second group includes three novels to date, written in French and published starting in 1995.

But there are at least two good reasons not to overestimate the importance of this linguistic division. The first is that, even though they are now available in Prague in their original language—after being initially issued in Canada by novelist couple Josef Škvorecký and Zdena Salivarová's Sixty-Eight Publishers, during the years when the books were proscribed in Czechoslovakia*— Kundera's Czech works are now French works as well, their French translations having been thoroughly revised by the author, who considers them as having "the same authenticity" as the originals. Does this linguistic transfer (the decision to abandon Czech for French and the "assimilation" into French of the novels written in

---

*Only *The Joke* and *Laughable Loves* were published in Prague while Kundera still lived there, the former in 1967 and the latter in 1970; the first editions of the five other novels written in Czech were first published in Paris in French translation between 1973 and 1990.

Czech) make Kundera a French novelist, as Guy Scarpetta says in his fine analysis of *Slowness*,* or does it at least make him a writer more "French" than he was already as the author of *Jacques and His Master* and *Farewell Waltz*, the reader of Rabelais and Vivant Denon? That, of course, is an unanswerable question. Probably the only way to respond with some accuracy is to repeat what Kundera himself said of his compatriot Vera Linhartová: "Is Linhartová still a Czech writer when she writes in French? No. Does she become a French writer? Not at all. She is elsewhere."† That is, where she has always been, in the country of her art.

The second reason not to harden the contrast between Kundera's Czech and French novels is that in doing so one risks not only ignoring or underestimating everything that links the latter to the former but also overestimating the continuity of the "Czech cycle" and missing the internal diversity that characterizes it.

This continuity is actually remarkable. Its most visible sign is not so much the use of the Czech language as it is a quite singular architectonic feature: the nearly obsessive recurrence of the number seven. That number not only governs the general design of the group (seven

---

*See Guy Scarpetta, "Divertimento à la française," in *L'Age d'or du roman* (Paris, 1996), pp. 253–70.
†"L'exil libérateur" (1994), in Chvatik, *Le Monde romanesque de Milan Kundera*, p. 254.

novels) but also the internal structure of each individual work in it, every one of them divided into seven parts, except for the central novel, *Farewell Waltz*, which has five; but the effect of this break from the consistency of the rule is to underscore it; it is, moreover, offset by the fact that the structure of *Farewell Waltz* echoes that of "Symposium," a narrative divided into five acts and also occupying a central position, within *Laughable Loves*. This sort of mathematical perfection confers such an equilibrium and cohesion upon Kundera's series of Czech novels that they can be taken for pieces of one and the same work, comparable in the scope of its composition and its magnificent realization to such novelistic cathedrals as Balzac's "Comédie humaine," Hermann Broch's *The Sleepwalkers*, Proust's *À la recherche du temps perdu*.

Even so it's possible, without losing sight of this unity, to discern within the Czech cycle two subgroups that are quite different in many ways. The first comprises the four novels written in Prague during the 1960s: *Laughable Loves* (whose various parts were written between 1959 and 1968); *The Joke* (completed in 1965); *Life Is Elsewhere* (1969); and *Farewell Waltz* (1971 or 1972).* The second consists of the Czech novels written

---

*Most of theese dates have been supplied by Kundera himself, either at the end of his novels or in Chvatik, *Le Monde romanesque de Milan Kundera*.

in Rennes and Paris between the late seventies and the late eighties: *The Book of Laughter and Forgetting* (completed in 1978), *The Unbearable Lightness of Being* (1982), and *Immortality* (1988).*

Although they should not be exaggerated, there really are differences between these two series of novels. Whereas the first four unfold in the same geographical and political setting, Czechoslovakia roughly between 1945 and 1970, the last three show a coming and going between Czechoslovakia on the one hand and "Western Europe" (France, Switzerland, the United States) on the other. Likewise, the use of a kind of situation comedy akin to farce is more frequent in the first period than in the second, where we find virtually nothing like Helena on the toilet in *The Joke,* Jaromil's undershorts in *Life Is Elsewhere,* or the erotic sparring between the young spa-magazine editor and Frantiska or between Eduard and the directress in *Laughable Loves.* The next three novels, on the other hand, give more space to essays and to sarcastic reflections on the contemporary world: graphomania in *The Book of Laughter and Forgetting,* kitsch in *The*

---

*In ibid., pp. 168–69, Chvatik proposes a different distribution of the seven Czech novels: on one side, the "anthropological, social, and philosophical novels" (*The Joke, Life Is Elsewhere, The Book of Laughter and Forgetting*); on the other, "works about love characterized by lightness of narrative" (*Laughable Loves, Farewell Waltz, The Unbearable Lightness of Being*); placed apart is *Immortality,* "a successful synthesis of motifs and themes from both groups."

Unbearable Lightness of Being, "imagology" in *Immortality*. And as to the characters: the most important figures in the earlier novels are men, some young (Eduard, Jaromil), some older (Ludvik, Havel, Jakub), whereas the second period sees the emergence of more developed female characters, whose positions in the novels are much more central than in the past: Tamina in *The Book of Laughter and Forgetting*, Tereza and Sabina in *The Unbearable Lightness of Being*, Agnès in *Immortality*.

More remarkable still is the thematic or climatic difference between the earlier and later Czech novels, a difference that can be described by repeating what was said in the preceding chapter about the novel of fighting and the novel of exile. *The Joke, Life Is Elsewhere*, and several parts of *Laughable Loves* derive from the adventure story, insofar as they recount the efforts and tribulations of characters spurred by the will to realize their desires and to conquer a world or overcome circumstances that seem hostile to them, characters who are prepared never to succeed and to end up dropping the fight; whereas *The Book of Laughter and Forgetting, The Unbearable Lightness of Being*, and *Immortality* are instead stories of defeat or abandonment, in which the essential part of the character's life takes place on or beyond the periphery of desire and adventure. The tranquillity, the melancholy passivity that colors the existence of a Tamina, for example, contrasts with the ambition and combativeness of a Ludvik or a Jaromil. In this respect *Farewell Waltz* marks a change: the three days Jakub spends in the small spa town are like a pause between his combative past and his coming emigration.

This thematic shift, moreover, is accompanied by a no less remarkable change of form. If it can indeed be said that Kundera's four earliest Czech novels, despite their incontestable originality, do not radically break with the great traditional novelistic conventions—unity of action, respect for chronology, dominance of a narrative style of discourse, and relative suppression of the narrator—the three following novels, by comparison, seem markedly more audacious, whether in their freedom from the habitual constraints of subject and form, in their fragmented narration, in the multiplicity and heterogeneity of the elements that enter into their composition, or in the presence of a particularly "active" narrator—all of them things certainly foretold by a novel like *Life Is Elsewhere*, but that in the three later novels written in Czech nonetheless assume new proportions.

Another way to demonstrate this difference is to use an expression of Kundera's and say that a novel worthy of the name simultaneously obeys two great principles, the "epic" (logical development of a story) and the "musical" (design of a form and development of a theme or group of themes). The first of these principles, from *Laughable Loves* to *Farewell Waltz*, is the most *conspicuous*, while the second, without, strictly speaking, being hidden, remains largely implicit, like a background that in order to be clearly seen requires some adjustment of sight. In *The Book of Laughter and Forgetting*, *The Unbearable Lightness of Being*, and *Immortality*, this arrangement is reversed: now it is the musical principle that stands in the foreground, and, without destroying the epic structure, subordinates it to the point of rendering it not exactly indiscernible but at least highly discontinuous, even spotty.

To illustrate this phenomenon, we need only compare *Farewell Waltz* and *The Book of Laughter and Forgetting*, the two works that lie on either side of the demarcation line and that, perhaps for this reason, exaggerate the characteristics of their respective "half-times" to their furthest limit. On one side a quasi-detective novel, its suspense managed by a masterly hand, in which the adventures and sudden turns, contained in a sharply circumscribed time and place, proceed with perfect logic, and whose narration stays within the thoughts and actions of a small group of characters who persist in remaining the same from beginning to end—in short, a story with a structure as concise, rigorous, and linear as that of a play. On the other side a work of entirely unexpected form, virtually unprecedented in the history of the novel, in which the plots succeed one another with no apparent connection, the settings and times keep changing, the characters remain enclosed in their respective stories and never cross paths, the heroine appears only once halfway through the novel, and the narration is often interrupted, torn apart by the novelist's memories and thoughts; and yet nothing—no scene, no character, no reflection—could be cut from *The Book of Laughter and Forgetting* without jeopardizing both the structure and each of its parts, whose meaning is directly inflected by the proximity of the others, like what occurs between the colors of a painting or the staves of a musical score.*

If this distinction I've just made is sound, there would thus be not one but two Czech cycles in Kundera's oeuvre, with the end of the first and the start of the second separated by a silence of six or seven years, the longest of his whole career. From the biographical point of view this silence coincides with the period when Kundera left Czechoslovakia and settled in France—a period, he says in *Testaments Betrayed,* when he believed his work was over:

> When I finished *Farewell Waltz,* at the very start of
> the 1970s, I considered my career as a writer over. It

---

*David Lodge puts forward an analogous comparison between *The Book of Laughter and Forgetting* and *The Joke* in *After Bakhtin: Essays on Fiction and Criticism* (London, 1990), pp. 154–67.

was under the Russian occupation and my wife and I had other worries. It wasn't until we had been in France a year (and thanks to France) that, after six years of a total interruption, I began without passion to write again. Feeling intimidated, and to regain my footing, I decided to tie into something I had already done: to write a kind of second volume of *Laughable Loves*. What a regression! . . . Fortunately, after drafting two or three of these "Laughable Loves II," I saw that I was writing an entirely different thing: not a story collection but a novel (later entitled *The Book of Laughter and Forgetting*). . . . At once, whatever mistrust I still harbored toward the art of the novel disappeared.

So, just as *Farewell Waltz* (whose title almost became *Epilogue*) is steeped in a mood of ending, *The Book of Laughter and Forgetting* marks a new departure in the novelist's career; that is, both a return or rebirth of the initial creative impulse and the discovery of new artistic means which his earlier oeuvre had harbored but hitherto had remained unexplored.

Indeed, it is because of a similar though probably less dramatic "crisis" and redeployment that, in the 1990s, after another six-year silence, a new cycle of works as utterly unexpected as the previous one came to be. This is what Kundera himself wrote in 1995:

With *Immortality*, I exhausted all the possibilities of a form that until then had been mine and that I had varied and developed since my first novel. Suddenly, this was clear: either I had reached the end of the road as a novelist or I was going to discover still another completely other road. Whence, too, the irresistible desire to write in French. To find myself completely elsewhere. On an unsuspected route. The change of form was as radical as that of language.*

In the three novels that so far constitute Kundera's French cycle—*Slowness* (completed in 1994), *Identity* (1996), and *Ignorance* (1999)—the most visible signs of formal change are the abandonment of the division into (seven or five) parts and, of course, their brevity; that is, the temporal tightening of the action and concentration on a relatively limited number of themes and characters as well as a still stronger wish to bring the "epic" and the "musical" principles into a tight bond. The broad and complex composition of the Czech novels, which can be compared to sonata form, is thus succeeded by the intimate and measured universe of the fugue. At the same time the group of three French novels is in a way bringing about a synthesis of the two preceding cycles. *Slowness*, for example, resounds anew with the

*Kundera, "La Bonne humeur," written dialogue with Guy Scarpetta, *La Règle du jeu* (May 1995).

"satanic" laughter of *Laughable Loves* and *Life Is Elsewhere*, softened by the nostalgic lightness of *Farewell Waltz*. Likewise, Chantal, in *Identity*, is a sister of Tereza and Agnès. As for *Ignorance*, whose main action takes place in Bohemia, one can't help but see it as a prolonging of the meditation on exile and memory, themes whose ramifications extend throughout the oeuvre, from *The Joke* and *Farewell Waltz* to *The Book of Laughter and Forgetting* and *The Unbearable Lightness of Being*. Spareness, concentration, purity of form, concern for the "essential structures" of existence—these features draw together Kundera's French trilogy and what Hermann Broch, particularly apropos Stravinsky and Picasso, considered the highest accomplishment of contemporary art, which he praised by simply calling it the *style of old age*.

A Single Book

So the map of the Kundera massif, as it might now be drawn, would seem to be divided into three zones in rather sharp relief: the first Czech cycle (a tetralogy spaced out over ten years), the second Czech cycle (a trilogy also spread over ten years), and a still-incomplete French cycle (three novels in five years). Although they follow one another in time, it would nonetheless be giving in to an optical illusion to consider these different cycles from a historical or "Darwinian" angle—that is, as a series of stages whereby, in more or less radical mutations and reconfigurations, a continuous process of transformation and of development was unfolding. There is no rupture, in fact, between the cycles in Kundera's oeuvre, no real "revolution." No one can say that *The Unbearable Lightness of Being* or *Immortality*, because they belong to the second cycle, are better novels, more "advanced" novels, or more "mature" novels than those of the preceding cycle, such as *The Joke* or *Life Is Elsewhere*. It's the same with the French novels: these works, even though late, are neither more nor less Kunderian than those that preceded them, and there is no need, in order to read them correctly, to have read the others.

In other words one can enter the Kundera massif through any portal and travel through it in any order. There are no "youthful novels" here, no "secondary works" or "transitional books," no changes of direction or sudden revelations in the course of the oeuvre, but, on the contrary, a constancy, an unfailing fidelity to itself— that is, to the initial moral and aesthetic vision with which this oeuvre began and then, with each cycle, with each new novel, only returns to that self and finds in it unexpected possibilities. That is why Kundera, recalling

Laughable Loves and the earliest beginning of his "novelist's path," could write in 1991: "From that moment on . . . starts my continuous literary evolution, which has certainly brought me a good many surprises but . . . no basic change in my aesthetic orientation."*

So one should relinquish the Hegelian perspective of "progress" if one wishes to understand the nature and role of the "cycles" in the long course of this oeuvre. Best would be to compare them to Picasso's "periods" ("blue," "rose," "African," and so on): not corrections of trajectory, not the repudiation or destruction of this or that in favor of something truer, more beautiful, or more right, but a series of variations within the same search or, better: within the same discovery, tirelessly pursued, tirelessly renewed. So, in this view, changing style, moving from one cycle to another, is not necessarily going farther or higher than before, leaving this area for that other larger one; on the contrary, it means staying in the territory one has chosen to occupy, but occupying it differently, altering one's observation posts, moving about in new directions so as to know it better and be still more at home in it.

That's why, in describing the whole of Kundera's

---

*Kundera, in Chvatik, *Le Monde romanesque de Milan Kundera*, p. 241; the novelist repeated this two years later: "In my evolution as a novelist there is no break between what I've written in Bohemia and what I've written in France" ("La 'parole' de Kundera," *Le Monde*, September 30, 1993).

work, I cling to that *geological* image of the massif, whose circularity and stability reduce the possibility of the linear and the falsely "evolutionary" in the division into cycles, which is certainly convenient, but dangerous when it leads to raising impenetrable barriers between works and groups of works that have much more in common than everything that would seem to separate them. As appropriate as the features we've used to characterize each of the three cycles seem, almost none, in fact, can be considered "distinctive"—that is, uniquely valid for one cycle but not for the others. Thus, the "epic" principle is *also*, of course, at work in the novels of the second Czech cycle, as is the "musical principle" in those of the first. Strong male characters are *also* to be found in *The Unbearable Lightness of Being* and *Immortality*, just as *The Joke* was already illuminated by the figure of Lucie, the older sister of Agnès and Tamina. Even the composition of the French novels, brief and with but a single theme, is not so remote from the composition that, in the Czech novels, launches each of the parts taken separately. In short, from one cycle to another there is no bifurcation or basic reorientation, but rather differences of emphasis, dominant features that shift, lines and plans that change their positions.

Thus Kundera's ten novels (and those to come) can—perhaps should—now be read as if they form a single "cycle," a single *circle* within which it is possible, from any point, to radiate out in all directions without ever leaving it. Read them, in other words, as if they were a single book, a Kundera book, of course—heterogeneous and varied, fresh on each page, and of which each page even as we read it continually refers us back to all the other pages and in our heads carries on a dialogue with them that alone allows the page we are reading to say all it has to. This method consists of dropping the "diachronic" approach by periods or by "cycles" in favor of reading works "in art's own time, with no upstream or downstream," of which Malraux speaks in *L' Homme précaire et la littérature,* and what E. M. Forster, for example, utilizes in examining the English-language novel since the eighteenth century: "Time, all the way through, is to be our enemy. We are to visualize the English novelists not as floating down that stream which bears all its sons away, . . . but as seated together in a room, a circular room, a sort of British Museum reading-room— all writing their novels *simultaneously*."* This is also a suitable way to consider Kundera's novels: whatever their order and date of composition, to imagine them as if they were written and as if we were reading them *simultaneously*, as if the massif they form stood whole before us, in this present reading that is his and ours both.

*E. M. Forster, *Aspects of the Novel* (New York: 1954), p. 21 (italics mine).

Paths (1):
Motifs, Themes, Characters

Reading a Balzac novel by chance is very different from living for a long time in the company of his oeuvre and little by little exploring the whole universe of the "Comédie humaine."

ALBERT BÉGUIN*

The most exact model for such "synchronic" reading, with neither upstream nor downstream, is once again Agnès, who teaches it to us when, after standing motionless to admire the vast panorama surrounding her, she initiates the second moment of her final afternoon in the mountains:

> She set out along a gentle path that led upward through meadows toward a forest.

*Albert Béguin, *Balzac lu et relu* (Paris: 1965), p. 41.

That moment, which continues for several hours, is that of the walk, of entry into the "world of paths," where contemplation of the landscape merges with its occupancy, knowing it with the walk—a lingering, thoughtful occupancy and walk, given over to the details and contours of the terrain and indifferent to any idea of progress, for paths know no time, have neither beginning nor end. "In the kind of forest loved by Agnès, paths branch into smaller paths, then into still smaller paths," which lead to other small paths, and those to a new path, which perhaps is the first one yet again or perhaps another—it's impossible to tell and it doesn't matter. A pure "tribute to space," a path functions not to cut through space, as a highway does, but to go over it at ground level, to merge with it and allow it to shift form with each step, each turn, each junction, for "every stretch of path has meaning in itself and invites us to stop." A highway is straight and singular; a path, by definition, is winding and part of a tangled, secret web: it neither advances nor retreats, but enjoys detours, crossings, forks, everything that reveals new ways between here and there, between this view and that, is pleased to backtrack, and literally go around in circles in that space which is not obstacle but domicile.

> Path and highway; . . . two conceptions of
> beauty. . . .
> In the world of highways, a beautiful landscape
> means: an island of beauty connected by a long line
> with other islands of beauty.
> In the world of paths, beauty is continuous and
> constantly changing; it tells us at every step: "Stop!"

It would probably be possible to approach Kundera's novels from the perspective of the highway, seeing them as so many separate "islands" or as successive stages of a (thematic and aesthetic) "development" continuing over time along "a line leading from one point to another" always "farther" than the preceding point. But that would be to betray Agnès, whom I do not want to leave for a single step. And it would risk losing sight of the "continuous and constantly changing beauty" of the Kunderian oeuvre, which only a sort of "path-reading" can give access to and experience fully: this *co-presence* in each novel, in each part or each chapter of each novel, of all the others at once, as the multiple perceptions of one self-same space that is constantly *unfolding*, of a totality not in progress but in continuous expansion, always the same and yet always new, always evident and always elusive.

In fact, one of the great pleasures of reading Kundera's oeuvre—as of reading any "oeuvre" worthy of the name—is this constant traffic it offers us: first within each novel, and from one novel to the next, and then to another and yet another, endlessly, as if each word, each character, nearly each scene we read were echoed in some other book, in connection with some other context, and gained extra meaning and complexity from it. To read, then, is not only to discover but also to recognize: to recognize in what we read something else we have read before and to prepare to recognize something we will soon be reading. It is to be perpetually in motion, here and elsewhere, here and downstream, here and upstream, impelled by connotations and recollections like the protean hat that saunters from novel to novel, each time bearing a new value, colored, completed, even contradicted by all the others associated with it elsewhere. Clementis's posthumous hat left behind on Gottwald's head and Papa Clevis's comic hat flung by the wind into Passer's open grave (*The Book of Laughter and Forgetting*); Beethoven and Goethe's immortal hats at the encounter with the Austrian empress (*Immortality*); the ridiculous motorcyclist's helmet on Vincent's resentful head (*Slowness*); Sabina's lewd bowler, which becomes "a motif in the musical composition" that is her life (*The Unbearable Lightness of Being*). All this headgear, all so various and yet all floating in the same air, ends up merging into one another to become, like the one we see on

Kafka or Chaplin, the Hat of a forever impenetrable enigma.

About Dogs

Many other things trace their paths across Kunderian space: the deceptive tablet swallowed in turn by Elisabet in "Symposium" (*Laughable Loves*), Helena in *The Joke*, and Ruzena in *Farewell Waltz*, bringing sleep or diarrhea to those who want to die, death to those who want to live. Then there is the harmonious setting, nostalgic and charged with sexual excitement, of the "small spa town" in which all of *Farewell Waltz* and at least one scene in nearly all the other novels take place; the moonlight that casts its mocking glimmer over the frolics of *Farewell Waltz*, "Symposium," and *Slowness*, making these tales a kind of triptych in the form of a nocturnal pantomime before bringing its pallid light, like "a forgotten lamp in the room of the dead," to the final pages of *The Unbearable Lightness of Being*; and the movie and television cameras, with their retinue of directors, journalists, and technicians who invade everywhere and make the same spectacle out of the life of a poet (*Life Is Elsewhere*), of an activist intellectual (*Slowness*), of a folklore festival (*The Joke*), of a political "Grand March" (*The Unbearable Lightness of Being*), of the privacy of bathing women (*Farewell Waltz*), and even of fetuses in their mothers' wombs (*Identity*).

From one novel to another, too, certain *scenes* echo whose structures are equivalent if not similar, and thus constitute, at the level of the entire oeuvre, kinds of narrative variations analogous to those that often govern the internal composition of each novel. One of the most frequent is the amorous relation between partners of different ages, be it an older man and a young woman (Kostka and Lucie, Bertlef and Ruzena, Jakub and Olga, the man in his forties and the young redhead, Paul and Laura), or the reverse (the lovers in "Let the Old Dead Make Room for the Young Dead"). A list of recurring scenes would also include betrayal by a friend (in *The Joke, Life Is Elsewhere, Farewell Waltz*); the orgy, a degraded form of the *fête galante* (in *Life Is Elsewhere, The Book of Laughter and Forgetting, Identity*); or a naked woman and a fully clothed man standing before a mirror (Helena and Ludvik, Sabina with Franz or Tomas, the "lute player" between Rubens and his friend, Gustaf and Irena's mother in *Ignorance*).

Marginal as they might seem, these recurrences nonetheless illustrate the phenomenon that interests us here: the existence beyond the particular universe of each novel of a wider, "border-spanning" universe in which words, motifs, or scenes, repeated from one novel to another, establish among them a multidirectional link of multiple meanings that has us, while reading one, partly rereading another, and thus makes our reading of each of them altered, complicated, and thus enriched by that fact.

One such motif to be found in nearly all the novels is that of the dog, as if this speechless creature from a universe unconcerned with the passions and destiny of human beings were always bringing them a message they cannot understand. Of course this motif fills an important role in *Farewell Waltz*, with the dog-hunt episode. Presaged in the book's "Second Day," it is narrated in detail in Chapter 7 of the "Third Day"—that is, in the *middle* of the novel, which gives it great significance, both dramatic (it is at the end of this scene, after saving a boxer, that Jakub conceives a "sudden, naked hatred" for Ruzena) and symbolic (this hunt is the degraded—and all the more terrible—image of the hunt for people that makes Jakub flee his country, the man/dog equivalence being confirmed within the novel by the fact that Dr. Skreta had been a dog breeder before he launched his human impregnation project). This entire semantic load, in *The Unbearable Lightness of Being*, is reactivated—and augmented—when Tereza learns that "all the dogs in a certain Russian city had been summarily shot," which reminds her of the time when her country was invaded by the Soviet army:

People were still traumatized by the catastrophe of the occupation, but radio, television, and the press went on and on about dogs: how they soil our streets and parks, endanger our children's health, fulfill no useful function, yet must be fed. . . . Only after a year did the accumulated malice (which until then had been vented, for the sake of training, on animals) find its true goal: people.

Since the hunt has been described in detail in *Farewell Waltz*, there is no need to do so again here; but its meaning, or one of its meanings, left implicit in the first account, can now be the subject of a commentary that would lack some of its power if we did not have in mind the central pages of *Farewell Waltz*.

Conversely, it can be said that all of Part Seven of *The Unbearable Lightness of Being* is like an expansion of a brief scene in *Farewell Waltz* that takes place soon after the dog hunt, when Jakub returns to its owners the boxer he has rescued. The proprietors of an inn outside the town, they are engrossed solely by their domestic happiness and love:

It was sunny outside, and the yellowing foliage bent gently over the open window. There was not a sound. The inn was well above the world, and one could find peace there.

The husband isn't named, the wife is called Vera; they could be called Tomas and Tereza. As for the dog, who answers to the name Bob, he is like a brother of Karenin, in *The Unbearable Lightness of Being*. But the basic effect of bringing these two scenes together is that it allows them to exchange their values and thus to illuminate their hidden ambiguity: the mortuary sadness of little Karenin and her (yes, *her*) masters is somehow brightened by the joyful liveliness of Bob and his family, which in return is tinged a little by the melancholy of the others.

A similar reverberation effect comes, in *Ignorance*, with the surreptitious appearance of another dog, a German shepherd, during Josef's visit to his friend N., who in the past had shielded him from certain political difficulties. If the joy with which the dog welcomes Josef allows, by contrast, a better understanding of N.'s uncomfortable attitude and his desire to forget, the dog's presence at the same time somehow comes to crystallize all the connections our reading has established, more or less consciously, from the start between this third of Kundera's French novels, the novel of the émigré's return, and *Farewell Waltz*, the novel of his departure. Friend of the German shepherd, Josef becomes the double of Jakub, friend and rescuer of Bob the boxer, and the similarity of their destinies, at once symmetrical and contradictory, as if one were merely a mirror image of the other, reverberates in their respective novels like one more question, bringing each book a heightened irony and beauty.

That said, the presence of the canine motif in *Ignorance* remains surreptitious. It is still more so in the other novels, such as *Life Is Elsewhere* (the images of dogs that haunt Jaromil's childhood dreams and drawings), *The Book of Laughter and Forgetting* (Karel's mama's poodle), or *Identity* (the beaten dog in the broom closet where Chantal takes refuge). And yet, every time it appears, and however brief its appearance, the motif has the power to prompt a kind of semantic leap toward the other parts of the oeuvre where it gets more sustained treatment.

As can be seen from the example of dogs (or hats), repetitions, as they occur in the whole oeuvre or within each individual novel, are governed by the same law that keeps them from being exact repetitions but rather, in fact, "variations," to use a term dear to Kundera. By virtue of that law, not only does the element always occur in varied contexts, which alter its value and connotations, but its treatment from one occurrence to another is also varied. At times it will be the only subject of a story or a meditation, both fairly well developed; at others it will be considered only briefly, as a secondary element within some other story or meditation; and finally at times it will only be a simple allusion, which the reader is free to linger over or disregard.

A Study of Rivers

If it is valid for the several motifs already noted, that law applies still more visibly to the great *themes* that, like rivers, flow through the whole expanse of the Kunderian oeuvre uninterrupted by any border, along the way picking up and spreading into each novel they irrigate an absolutely inexhaustible semantic silt. Many of these major themes are announced by the titles of the different novels or sections of novels that correspond to the place in the oeuvre where they undergo the most thorough or most concentrated "investigation." Let's enumerate, just to recall: *Laughable Loves, The Book of Laughter and Forgetting*, "The Border," "Soul and Body," "Words Misunderstood," "The Face," "Fighting," "Chance," *Slowness, Identity*. It may designate a very narrow segment of the oeuvre, but each of these titles is also a source and a confluence from which arise and to which flow multiple currents of meaning that link the novel or the novel section it designates to other, sometimes very remote, regions of the oeuvre and make the oeuvre, *in its totality*, the area of a literally endless exploration of those bottomless wells that are laughable love, laughter, forgetting, the border, identity. Let's make do here, as an example, with briefly following the course of some of these "trans-Kunderian" thematic rivers.

The Unbearable Lightness of Being. Though that theme gives its title to this particular novel, in which Parts One and Five are both called "Lightness and Weight" and in which it is most amply developed, it also runs beneath the surface in several other Kundera novels, as, by the way, he notes in *The Art of the Novel.* Dr. Havel in *Laughable Loves* has already made it one of the arguments in his monologue about the end of the "Don Juans": "Don Juan bore on his shoulders a dramatic burden that the Great Collector has no idea of, because in his world every burden has lost its weight." The same idea comes to Jakub's mind when, reflecting on the "murder" of Ruzena he has just committed, he compares himself to the hero of *Crime and Punishment*:

> Raskolnikov experienced his crime as a tragedy, and eventually he was overwhelmed by the weight of his act. Jakub was amazed that his act was so light, so weightless, amazed that it did not overwhelm him. And he wondered if this lightness was not more terrifying than the Russian character's hysterical feelings.

Ludvik, at the end of *The Joke*, also feels that burden without weight, that terrifying lightness, when, after hearing Kostka's revelations about Lucie's (and thus his own) past, he discovers in himself "the heavy lightness of the void that weighed on my life." And the image recurs in Part Six of *The Book of Laughter and Forgetting*, where its paradoxical nature is still more emphatic. No longer able to bear the burden of her memories, Tamina yields to Raphael's invitation to go "where things weigh nothing at all." But very soon after her arrival on the children's island, she feels growing within her, and consuming her, "the nausea that emanates from weightless things":

> That hollowness in her stomach is exactly that unbearable absence of weight. And just as an extreme can at any moment turn into its opposite, so lightness brought to its maximum becomes the terrifying *weight of lightness.*

From a strictly diachronic point of view, the presence of such passages in the novels preceding *The Unbearable Lightness of Being* would appear to be merely a simple prefiguration of the novel to come—that is, a series of stages marking the process of its fairly early "genesis." But from our perspective—the perspective of the massif, of time with no up- or downstream—each of these passages, on the contrary, possesses full value in itself. Act-ing as a kind of aperture, it introduces into *Laughable Loves*, into *The Joke*, or into *The Book of Laughter and Forgetting* all the richness and all the complexity of the theme, that is, the whole interrogation bound to lightness and weight that comprises the material of *The Unbearable Lightness of Being*. Through Havel's or Ludvik's remarks, through Tamina's thoughts, we hear the voices, we have the experiences, of Tomas and Tereza, of Sabina and Franz, which in return also mingle with those of their distant companions.

In the very middle of Part Five of *Immortality*, there occurs this dialogue between the novelist and his friend, Professor Avenarius, who asks:

> "And what will your novel be called?"
> "*The Unbearable Lightness of Being*."
> "I think somebody has already written that."
> "I did! But I was wrong about the title then. That title was supposed to belong to the novel I'm writing right now."

This title could, in fact, belong to all of Kundera's novels.

Identity. This is another title that also suits all of them. "What is an individual?" Kundera writes in *Testaments Betrayed*. "Wherein does his identity reside? All novels seek to answer these questions." In his own novels, the enigma essentially takes the form of doubt, of that constant "wonder at the uncertain nature of the self and of its identity" that evokes *The Art of the Novel,* wonder that makes up another of the thematic rivers whose course we can follow through each of the novels, in the lives of nearly all the characters. I'm not going to do that here, but only ask a question: Would we understand Chantal, the heroine of *Identity,* as well as we do if her experience of the fragility and of the impossible stability of her self were not echoed by the experiences, in other parts of the oeuvre, of characters who in no way resemble her but who also run up against the same enigma— which is a source of anguish for some people, of freedom for others, of perplexity for all?

The revelation—or the distress—can occur at any moment, and transform "a stable and distinct being," as Alice, the girlfriend of the hero of "Eduard and God," initially appears to him to be, into a kind of gangling marionnette, a pure "inorganic conjunction, arbitrary and unstable," of a soul and body come apart, strangers to each other and capable, each of them, of all kinds of metamorphoses. It happens to Jean-Marc with Chantal, and it happens to the young man of "The Hitchhiking Game," when his fiancée suddenly seems "hopelessly *other*, hopelessly *alien*, hopelessly *polymorphous.*"

It was as if he were looking at two images through the same lens, at two images superimposed one on the other with one showing through the other. These two images showing through each other were telling him that *everything* was in the girl, that her soul was terrifyingly amorphous, that it held faithfulness and unfaithfulness, treachery and innocence, flirtatiousness and chastity. This disorderly jumble seemed disgusting to him, like the variety to be found in a pile of garbage.

What the young man doesn't see is that the same "disorderly jumble" also rules in him, within his own self, and that he himself, as Ludvik, in *The Joke,* discovers, has "many faces" among which it is impossible to distinguish a "real face [from] several false ones," because they were all "real," that is, the ones just as evanescent and illusory as the others. Such would be, in *Immortality*, the great discovery by Agnès, heroine par excellence of the "loss of identity." Since the death of her father, Agnès's existence has been one long project of demolition, in herself, of all the features by which an "I" claims to define a self, that is, a unique being who both differs from everyone else and keeps the same identity in all circumstances. The name, the face, the gestures that are supposedly one's own—all these things she soon comes to see as the effects of mere chance, random tatters. At the very beginning of the novel, she tells Paul:

> It must have happened some time toward the end of my childhood: I kept looking in the mirror for such a long time that I finally believed that what I was seeing was my self. My recollection of this period is very vague, but I know that the discovery of the self must have been intoxicating. Yet there comes a time when you stand in front of a mirror and ask yourself: this is my self? And why? Why did I want to identify with *this*? What do I care about this face? And at that moment everything starts to crumble. Everything starts to crumble.

To understand Chantal's anguish is to hear from afar, beyond the walls of the room in which she lies awake beside Jean-Marc, and through the whole space of Kundera's oeuvre, the sound of that crumbling.

Slowness. Polysemous, even ambiguous, a Kunderian theme is the opposite of a "sign"; it has no stable referent by which it can be replaced and thus undone. On the contrary, its nature is never to allow any but approximate and provisional deciphering. It is not meant to be "decoded"—that is, mastered—but to be endlessly explored and interrogated. For its connotations, its semantic "valences," like those of a poem, are quite unlimited, and any "understanding of which," as the author of *The Book of Laughter and Forgetting* says, "recedes . . . into the distance." A theme has neither a right nor a wrong side, neither a specific nor a figurative meaning, neither truth nor falseness. It can convey all values, none more correct or profound than the others. So when Jan and Edwige differently interpret a theme from *Daphnis and Chloe*, or when Franz and Sabina, in *The Unbearable Lightness of Being*, ascribe contradictory content to the "words misunderstood" that both unite and separate them, neither is more right than the other; as incompatible as they seem, their interpretations only illustrate the "infinite diversity of the interior world" that lies concealed in the theme and determines that we never know it completely, that we must constantly return to it, repeat it, rediscover it.

What, for example, is slowness? In Kundera's first French novel, it is associated with memory, grace, and pleasure "rationally organized, mapped out, delineated, calculated, measured." "Queen of reason," "guardian of happiness," Madame de T. "possesses the wisdom of slowness and deploys the whole range of techniques for slowing things down." Similar values are to be found in Part Five of *Immortality*, when Agnès, in the mountains, again takes up the "world of paths," slow, old, inhabited by the verses of Rimbaud and Goethe; but eroticism is no longer what the slowness of that world evokes in Agnès's mind; instead it evokes the memory of her father and, through that, solitude and death. Nor is there much epicurean connotation to the "melancholy slowness" that Ludvik, the hero of *The Joke*, finds in the young woman he has just met:

> Yes, it must have been Lucie's singular slowness that fascinated me, a slowness radiating a resigned consciousness that there was nowhere to hurry to and that it was useless to reach impatiently toward anything.

The emblem of "reason" and indispensable ornament of love's choreography for Madame de T., the effect of resignation (or, as we discover later, of the fear of love) in Lucie, the same slowness (the *same?*) becomes in Flajsman, the young man of "Symposium," one of the attributes of immaturity, which "testified far more to his nonchalant self-love than to clumsiness, [this] self-love [with which] the young intern would gaze attentively into his own heart, disregarding the insignificant details of the outside world."

What, in the end, is slowness?

The agreement with being. The last of the Kunderian rivers we will be traveling down differs somewhat from the previous ones in that any discussion of it cannot easily be organized around a novel or section of a novel that would be its source or the point of its greatest clarity. Although it is as constant as the others, it is a broader river, with many abundant tributaries, whose alluvial deposits do not form so much a particular theme—that is, some word or group of words—as a kind of "arch-theme," more vast and general, whose variously named manifestations are all similar in structure and share—to continue our river metaphor—an immense common semantic basin.

Playing a role in Kundera's oeuvre—and in his intellectual and aesthetic universe—analogous to that of *vanity* in Stendhal or *stupidity* in Flaubert, this arch-theme, if it must after all be designated by a single word, would probably best be called *innocence*, a typically Kunderian category of the "romantic lie." Innocence as existential attitude and as vision of the world, as position and as program, whose essence resides at once in the irrepressible need for harmony, purity, the absolute, its positive side, and—its negative side (it's the same thing)—in disregard or concealment of any conflict and any contradiction. Such, we may recall, is the definition of kitsch in Part Six of *The Unbearable Lightness of Being*:

> Kitsch is the absolute denial of shit, in both the literal and the figurative senses of the word; kitsch excludes everything from its purview which is essentially unacceptable in human existence [negative side]. . . . Kitsch has its source in the categorical agreement with being [positive side].

"The categorical agreement with being": another way of describing the innocence of someone who, confronted by the world and his own identity, perceives no flaw, no uncertainty, no insurmountable obstacle, not a single shadow projected onto them by error, shit, or death. But innocence has many faces. They define kitsch, but these same words also actually apply, in Kundera's oeuvre, to other manifestations of the same attitude. To lyricism, for instance, in *Life Is Elsewhere*: "By means of a poem, man achieves his agreement with being"; or, in *The Book of Laughter and Forgetting*, to the "serious laughter," to the "ecstatic laughter" of Gabrielle and Michelle, "the expression of being rejoicing in being" that proclaims to the whole world: "We're happy, we're glad to be in the world, we're in agreement with being!" Or again, in the same novel, to music "returned to its primeval state," pouring out everywhere from electric guitars and even burying beneath its joyful stupidity the last sighs of the dying:

> Everyone can fraternize by means of these simple combinations of tones, for it is being itself that through them is shouting out its jubilant "I'm here!" There is no more boisterous, no more unanimous agreement than the agreement with being.

Under the various metamorphoses it submits to, this feeling, this need for "agreement with being," is throughout Kundera's oeuvre a subject of privileged meditation, about which one of the great discoveries might rightly be expressed like this: the domain of innocence, of lyrical blindness and of kitsch is boundless. "For none among us," writes the author of *The Unbearable Lightness of Being*, "is superman enough to escape kitsch completely. No matter how we scorn it, kitsch is an integral part of the human condition."

One of its most "studied" variants—revealed, in fact by Kundera—is of course the political one, particularly (but not uniquely) totalitarian, that is, the not accidental but necessary link between innocence and oppression: if the poet reigns along with the hangman, as *Life Is Elsewhere* depicts, it is because they absolutely need each other, for the only real (and effective) hangman is an innocent hangman. Innocence—the sense of behaving "in agreement" with the crowd and in history's direction—is the engine of every revolution, of every struggle, whatever it may be. In *The Joke* that innocence is called "Joy" with a capital *J*: "a grave joy that proudly called itself 'the historical optimism of the victorious class,' a solemn and ascetic joy" which Helena, among others, has made the theme of her life; in *The Book of Laughter and Forgetting*, it takes form in the image of the angels' "ring dance"; in *The Unbearable Lightness of Being*, in the myth of the "Grand

March," in which is expressed "the political kitsch joining leftists of all times and tendencies."

But the angelicism of the militant (and of the hangman) is only one of the innumerable masks of innocence,
which is also at work in the thousand and one forms of
romantic love, in the "hypertrophy of the soul" from
which *Homo sentimentalis* suffers, in the thirst for glory
and the "longing for immortality," in the lofty words
("life," "future," "hope") that advertising and imagology
use to conceal human misery, in the euphoria of forgetting,
in ecstasy, in youth: wherever failure and imperfection are
ignored, shit hidden, the devil's laughter supplanted by
acceptance and the "spirit of poetry."

In fact innocence all the more prevails, and its avatars
are all the more numerous and rich as it corresponds to
everything by which the Kunderian novel very precisely
defines itself or seeks to define itself against. To return to
it constantly, never to tire of proliferating its variations
and seeking their meaning, is, for the novelistic imagination, to contemplate as in a mirror its own reversed reflection, its exact antithesis, and thus constantly to learn to
know itself better and keep track of what brought it to
birth and can keep it what it is.

Balzac's Strategy

Thus from one end to the other of the Kunderian massif, the recurrence of motifs, scenes, and themes weaves a vast "hypertextual" canvas whose role recalls that played, in the "Comédie humaine," by the famous technique of the reappearance of characters, an agent for both unity and diversity—unity *within* diversity and diversity *within* unity. Indeed, not only does this technique throw footbridges between the Balzacian novels that open them up by making them look like parts of a single universe capable of containing them all, but the character, in moving about inside this "transnovelistic" universe, acquires a kind of ontological independence that increases his credibility and, above all, makes him or her both more complex and more mysterious. Thus, over the course of *La Peau de chagrin*, *Père Goriot*, *La Maison Nucingen*, and *Splendeurs et misères des courtisanes*—that is, through his successive appearances at different ages and settings—Rastignac grows even wealthier and more problematic, and thereby escapes the slightly monolithic simplicity that sometimes threatens the Balzac characters.

Imitated since the nineteenth century by some of the best as well as the worst novelists, Balzac's strategy does not occur as such in Kundera's oeuvre, in which no character, properly speaking, moves from one novel to another. The only case that would approach it somewhat is that of Jaromil, the hero of *Life Is Elsewhere*, who is mentioned by name in Part Three of *Immortality*; but it is merely a reference to an earlier book by the novelist, not a character's new entrance on the scene, in the Balzac manner. Nowhere, in fact, does Kundera resort to this procedure, and in this regard each of his novels is truly enclosed on itself and on the fictional population that inhabits it. No Vautrin, no Angelo, no Nathan Zuckerman here crosses the borders of the novel in which he appears.

Which doesn't mean—far from it—that Kunderian characters are complete strangers to one another or are "snuffed out" for good on the last page of their respective novels. Rather the opposite: however unique and strongly individualized he or she is, nearly every character here has, somewhere in the oeuvre, another existence, indeed several other existences; they are born anew, live anew, experience new adventures, and thus constantly reveal unknown features. In other words Kundera's oeuvre also resorts to the "Balzac strategy" and finds in it a means of communication among the novels that comprise it. But it does this in a different manner: not, properly speaking, by the return of the *character* as such, identified by the permanence of a name and the continuity of a fate, but by the return of the plural creature I shall call, for lack of a better term, the "figure."

More general than the character, but less disembodied than the "type," the figure is a category at once abstract and concrete. Abstract in that it collects within the same family or the same "species" (to speak again in Balzac's language) a number of characters each with a name and a history but possessing certain features in common. And concrete in that a figure thus meant cannot be understood apart from the particular existence of each and every one of the characters that embody it, altogether or partly, constantly or occasionally, essentially or accidentally.

For instance, how can we not be struck by the presence of all those characters who threaten or attempt suicide? Much more frequent than those who actually kill themselves, who remain few (Alexej in *The Joke*, Stalin's son in *The Unbearable Lightness of Being*), the figure of the *suicidal* does recur in almost all the Kundera novels and is always female. This is sometimes touching (Tamina in *The Book of Laughter and Forgetting*, Milada in *Ignorance*, the girl in Part Five of *Immortality*), sometimes laughable (Helena in *The Joke*, Elisabet in *Laughable Loves*, Laura in *Immortality*, Immaculata in *Slowness*), and nearly always both at once.

Another figure still more typically Kunderian: that of the *banished* person, that is, of those whose actions or circumstances have deprived them of their status and caused them to "fall" from their destinies, like Ludvik, like Tomas and Tereza after their return from Switzerland, like Eduard's brother in *Laughable Loves*, and like the man in his forties in *Life Is Elsewhere*. All are fallen creatures, but all, paradoxically, find at the depths of their disgrace an unexpected peace, just as the Czech scientist in *Slowness* realizes in reflecting on the period when he lost his position and became a workman:

> He remembers when he and his mates would go swimming after work in a little pond behind the construction site. To tell the truth, he was a hundred times happier then than he is today in this château. The workmen used to call him Einstein, and they were fond of him.

An analogous figure, a variant of the preceding one, would be that of the stateless person, the exile. Such are Jan in *The Book of Laughter and Forgetting*, Josef in *Ignorance*, and even Jakub in *Farewell Waltz*, who is on his way to emigration. Also exiled are Sabina (*The Unbearable Lightness of Being*), Tamina (*The Book of Laughter and Forgetting*), and Irena (*Ignorance*). Proscribed within or driven out of their country, these banished and exiled characters are most often solitary creatures as well, separate, without bonds. Whether they are unmarried, widowed, divorced, it is as if they had broken every contract with others and were living both cut off from and free of any community, withdrawn—rejected—in their single, private existence.

Despite their kinship and the similarity of their destinies, the characters we can group under the same figure are not of course simply clones of one another. Each has a particular way and reasons to be what he is, each has a history, an "existential code" that belongs to him alone. But each, at the same time, is a brother of the others, and through his reflection in their experience, his own becomes better known, subject to ever new interpretations, and at the same time, is somewhat lightened. The presence of these recurrent figures is basically only another case, another "application" of the Kunderian *variation* technique: like other meanings, a character's significance is never stable and thus cannot be grasped at once ("*Einmal ist keinmal*"—what happens only once might as well not have happened). It requires that we incessantly come back to it, that the character be reborn at once different and the same, that he plunge back into life, which is both his snare and his revelation, to the point where our understanding of him, and of the theme, ultimately "recedes into the distance."

This technique explains—and requires—that the Kunderian character always retains something a bit schematic or abstract. In this regard he is quite distinct from the realistic character in the Balzac mold, whose individuality is strongly marked: his name, his titles, his personality, his past, the least of his habits, just like every detail of his body, his clothes, his living conditions, are revealed to the reader. In Kundera we find no portrait of this sort, the characters tending on the contrary to maintain a kind of generality or anonymity. We know a character's gender, age, profession, entry in the state registry—that is, the basic determinants of his situation in the world—but the singularity of his *person* is largely erased: there is no family name, sometimes not even a given name; his physical attributes and facial features are not described, no more than his apartment or the city he lives in, which often go without a name or precise location. Stripped of everything picturesque that would differentiate him, defined primarily by what might be called his basic existential marks—the very ones that make up the "figure"—each character can then be seen as one of the multiple possibilities, one of the variations of that single figure thus made new and kept ever familiar.

Among these "variations on character," one of the most developed is the figure of the young man (or sometimes young woman). Like a Balzac character, he actually "returns" in practically every one of the novels, endowed with a different name and identity but always personified by the same inexperience and energy, that is, by the same absolute faith in himself and the same search for a "comforting, boundless, redeeming embrace, which would save him from the horrifying relativity of the freshly discovered world." In *The Joke*, for example, he is the Ostrava barracks commander and also Jindra, Helena's toady; in *Laughable Loves*, Flajsman and Havel's young editor disciple; in *Farewell Waltz*, poor Frantisek; in *The Book of Laughter and Forgetting*, they are Madame Raphael's girl pupils and the student victim of *litost*, "a state of torment" that is "one of the ornaments of youth"; in *Immortality*, Brigitte, Paul's beloved daughter, and Bettina, proud of being "part of the young generation . . . distinguished by Romanticism and [eye]glasses"; in *Ignorance*, Josef, finding himself back (and no longer recognizing himself) in the young "snot" who long ago wrote his high-school diary.

But two characters stand out among the prototypes of the Kunderian young man: Jaromil, to be sure, whose entire brief existence is merely the concrete "experimentation," by means of the novel, of "that period when a person has no need to enter the world because he is a world unto himself"; and Vincent, the young hero of *Slowness*. If Vincent's blindness before Julie's nakedness replicates Flajsman's before Elisabet's body, if his reaction to the suggestion of the man in the three-piece suit tends toward *litost*, if his way of imitating Pontevin recalls the young editor in *Laughable Loves*, Vincent still most resembles Jaromil. A devotee of metaphors, a narcissistic rebel and anguished lover, endowed like Jaromil, who battles "a strange mocking clown between his legs," with a talking penis that does whatever it wants, Vincent too fails to understand that "*to show himself* to the world is an entirely different thing from *going into* the world" and coming to terms with it. It's true that the worlds in which the two young men live— the "traps" that are set for them—are not at all the same. Unlike the Prague of 1948, the posthistorical universe of imagologues and "dancers" no longer has any weight, the hangmen have been discharged, from now on everything there has become inconsequential, and the very possibility of the tragic has disappeared. Vincent is no longer in a world one can "enter" or "go into," since there is no more world, no longer anything that resists, no more "life elsewhere." So nothing is left for him from now on but to stare at his own image and, finding nothing there, to "show himself" pathetically, frantically, at the cost of all the humiliations turned into "ceremonial trumpet fanfares" and into protests against all sorts of things.

Where does it come from, this fascination with the figure of the young person, which makes Kundera's oeuvre, along with Gombrowicz's, one of the most thoughtful and devastating "studies" of that modern myth par excellence that is youth? Characters in novels, writes the author of *The Unbearable Lightness of Being*, explore "a basic human possibility that the author thinks no one else has discovered or said something essential about." Indeed the "basic situation of immaturity" is precisely one of these possibilities, or rather: it is a situation all the richer in unexplored human possibilities because of the fact that it is eclipsed by tons of poetry, of lofty ideas, and of soothing images. If it hopes to reveal the world, the novel cannot refuse to make the young man's innocence and sovereignty one of its most important subjects—or targets.

But there is still another reason. There exists, between the young man and the modern novel of the "Hegelian type," a nearly mandatory natural alliance. "Young people especially," Hegel writes about literary heroes, "are these modern knights who must force their way through the course of the world which realizes itself instead of their ideals," so that they regard it as "cruelly [opposing] the ideals and the infinite rights of the heart." The age of ideals, the age of rebellion and struggle, youth, like kitsch, thus becomes for the Kunderian novel a kind of antiterritory, the realm against which, or standing aloof from which, it seeks to build its own realm, unillusioned

and marked with the "mature virility" and the "melancholy of the adult state" so well described by Lukács."*
A novelist," Kundera has confided, "is always born atop the demolished homestead of his own lyricism"†—in other words: of his youth, of that "radiant young faith" (Lukács) in himself that has him believe the world is his to dispose of. Directing attention toward the young man figure, reinventing it tirelessly, contemplating it from every angle, and laughing at it is therefore, for the novelist, to "demolish" it again and constantly to reenact the birth of his art, to return to the distance, the aging, the "sidestep" that makes him what he is.

One of the most characteristic features of the young man is that he is in love. Or rather: it is the way he is in love that makes him the exact antithesis of that other important Kunderian figure: the *libertine*, also known as the womanizer, the chaser, or, to cite Dr. Havel of "Symposium," the Great Collector—in short, he who, like Rubens in *Immortality*, locates "his life's center of gravity . . . not in public life but in private, not in the pursuit of professional success but in success with women." Besides the experience that he owes to his age—he is generally in his forties, like Martin in *Laughable Loves*, Jan in *The Book of Laughter and Forgetting*, or the hero of Part Six of *Life Is Elsewhere*, or even

The Theory of the Novel, pp. 85–86.
†Interview with Jean-Pierre Salgas, *La Quinzaine littéraire* (August 1984).

in his sixties, like Bertlef or the same Havel "after twenty years"—everything about this character stands in contrast with the young man, beginning, of course, with his view and practice of love. Far from "*love-emotion*" (*Immortality*), which is always only self-admiration in the, in effect, nonexistent face and body of the other, far from "*romantic* obsession" with the unique, ideal woman (*The Unbearable Lightness of Being*), and, above all, far from those few key words that define love for the virgin boy: "ecstasy," "life together," "faithfulness," "true passion"; the libertine, like Martin, daily plucks "the golden apple of eternal desire," of that manifold and ever-new desire kindled in him by the inexhaustible presence and charm of all women here, in the world, with whom can be shared the delights of seduction, conquest, and mutual sensual pleasure. Where the young man, "that scatterbrain," is himself "incapable of being satisfied with a beautiful *moment*" because "a beautiful moment was meaningful to him only if it was an emissary from a beautiful eternity," as is said in *Life Is Elsewhere,* the libertine on the contrary cultivates amours with no tomorrow and which for that reason he makes into a bunch of small masterpieces. For there is no better lover than that passionless Boccaccian "misogynist." Expert in erotic maneuvers and games, self-controlled, enemy of lofty words and feelings, and suspicious of any *overstuffed* significance, he is a lover entirely focused on his "prey" of the moment, his partner, his girlfriend whom he cherishes for what she is, soul and body, desirable and fragile, as imperfect as existence itself.*

Thus its "objectivity" is what distinguishes the libertine attitude most strongly from what, toward the end of *The Joke*, Ludvik calls "that stupid *lyrical age*, when a man is too great a riddle to himself to be interested in the riddles outside himself and when other people (no matter how dear) are mere walking mirrors in which he is amazed to find his own emotions, his own worth." The libertine, on the contrary, is a creature of minimal subjectivity, entirely engrossed by the people and events of the external world, and his "conquest" enterprise is the least egocentric, the most extroverted there is, seeing that it consists of giving oneself body and soul, so to speak, to objects outside himself that entice him by their resistance, their novelty, and what Tomas, in *The Unbearable Lightness of Being*, calls their "endless variety." "Speaking for myself," says Molière's Don Juan, "beauty enchants me wherever I find it and . . . I feel I could love the whole world."† Love, that is to say discover, explore, be driven, like Tomas, "not for [sexual] pleasure (the pleasure came as an extra, a bonus) but for

*On this subject, see Eva Le Grand's fine analyses in *Kundera ou la Mémoire du désir* (Paris and Montreal, 1995).
†Molière, *Don Juan*, 1.2, in *The Miser and Other Plays,* trans. John Wood and David Coward (New York, 1953; reprint, 2000), pp. 98–99.

possession of the world (slitting open the outstretched body of the world with his scalpel)." Don Juanism, in short, is a form of *knowledge*. And that is why we can say that whereas youth is naturally a poet, the libertine's art form is the novel.

Just as young-man lyricism may effectively be contrary to the spirit of the Kunderian novel, so the libertine's "satanic" consciousness is the novel's emblem or its model distillation, which explains the special attachment the novelist displays toward that figure—both in the loyalty that constantly draws him back to it and in his "affectionate" treatment of it—an affection all the greater for its element of nostalgia, given the increasing unlikelihood of such a character in our "daddified" world where men, as the heroine of *Identity* observes, have stopped turning to look at women. For Kundera, rescuing the libertine is rescuing the novel. Because with his "cold eye," with the detachment and "radical nonadherence" that defines the libertine, as Guy Scarpetta has noted,* but also, I would add, with the capricious, playful, essentially transitory and non-linear (or non-Hegelian) nature of his adventures, joined to the ironic consciousness he has about himself and his presence in the world ("I am at most a figure of comedy," Havel declares), the libertine (or his unromantic mistress:

*Guy Scarpetta, *L' Impureté* (Paris, 1985), p.275.

Sabina, Madame de T., the "lute player" in *Immortality*) embodies in his way the wisdom and aesthetic of the novel.

In any case, nothing better illuminates this Kunderian method of bringing back characters—or, more precisely, *figures* of characters—than seeing at work in it that same "libertine obsession," that same hunger to know, that same "strategy" which flings Tomas, for example, into the pursuit of women, of whom he has had "two hundred, give or take a few." "What did he look for in them?" the novelist asks. "What attracted him to them? Isn't making love merely an eternal repetition of the same?" We can ask this question about the characters. All those young men, those exiles, those skirt chasers (not to mention the Zemaneks, Cechackovas, Bernard Bertrands, Leroys, Bercks, and so on, all of them worthy representatives of the Molièresque figure of the "complete ass"), all those people who can seem cast from the same mold, like Dr. Skreta's kids—aren't they basically the same character, don't they too only imitate, repeat one another indefinitely?

> Not at all [the author of *The Unbearable Lightness of Being* responds]. There is always the small part that is unimaginable. . . . Using numbers, we might say that [in human beings] there is one-millionth part dissimilarity to nine hundred ninety-nine thousand nine hun-

dred ninety-nine millionth parts similarity. Tomas was obsessed by the desire to discover and appropriate that one-millionth part; he saw it as the core of his obsession. He was not obsessed with women; he was obsessed with what in each of them is unimaginable, obsessed, in other words, with the one-millionth part that makes a woman dissimilar to others of her sex.

Repetition—the return of a figure—is never just a repetition; it is the never finished, never abandoned search for each character's difference and unique identity. Tomas's obsession, in short, is an obsession with variation.

Paths (2): Composition

Writing without fabricating suspense, without constructing a plot and working up its plausibility . . . writing without describing a period, a milieu, a city . . . abandoning all that and holding on to only the essential.

MILAN KUNDERA

During one of his conversations with Professor Avenarius, "Mr. Kundera," the author of *Immortality*, castigates novels constructed in such a way, he says, that they are a "mad chase after a final resolution":

> I love Alexandre Dumas. . . . All the same, I regret that almost all novels ever written are much too obedient to the rules of unity of action. What I mean to say is that at their core is one single chain of causally related acts and facts. . . . Dramatic tension is the real curse of the novel, because it transforms everything, even the most beautiful pages, even the most surpris-

ing scenes and observations merely into steps leading
to the final resolution, in which the meaning of everything that preceded is concentrated.

"A novel," Avenarius's friend adds, "shouldn't be like
a bicycle race but like a banquet of many courses." A
banquet—or a "feast," as Fielding calls it at the beginning of *Tom Jones*—that is, a series of varied and delicious moments each having its own value and succeeding
one another without haste, with no purpose but to pro-
long enjoyment, to occupy time while suspending it, and
through their sequence make connections, variously close
or remote, among colors, textures, and flavors that the
guest discovers as they appear before him. A banquet,
also, in the Platonic tradition, a conversation, a "symposium," the sharing of serious or frivolous remarks
devoted to nothing more than delight and the preserva-
tion of harmony, and thus free of all polemical or
explanatory intentions, of all pressure toward a conclusion, welcoming, on the contrary, the repartee and non
sequiturs that, while keeping the exchange open, set it
moving in unexpected directions.

The master of ceremonies in Kundera's oeuvre is
Bertlef, the first-generation American in *Farewell Waltz*,
whose entire existence, now that he knows his days are
numbered (and perhaps for that reason), is a series of

last suppers and friendly discussions aimed at enhancing life and enjoying the "unforeseeable"; an existence that neither pursues nor flees anything, thereby distinguishing itself from that of other characters—Klima, Jakub, Skreta—all of whom have a project to accomplish, a mistake to correct, and thus nothing more pressing than to reach their objectives. A novel that would resemble "a banquet of many courses" would be a novel written by and for Bertlef.

Or else a novel written by and for Tamina, who is the "principal character and [the] principal audience" of *The Book of Laughter and Forgetting*. Here too the author expresses the desire to abandon the novel based on unity of action and dramatic tension, a form like the symphony, that "musical epic [of which] we might say that it is like a voyage leading from one thing to another, farther and farther away through the infinitude of the exterior world." In its place, he imagines "a novel in the form of variations" that would also be a kind of voyage, but "into the . . . infinitude . . . of the interior world," that is, a circular voyage, a nearly motionless one, where the important thing would not be to go constantly and as rapidly as possible from a cause to its effect, from one action to the next action, where the reader would not be condemned to "move forward," eating up kilometers and kilometers of plot before the impending arrival of the final revelation, but where he would be constantly stimulated to concentrate, to question a truth that is both enduring and always delayed, always elsewhere and always here, before his eyes, dazzling with presence and obscurity. In the interior voyage among variations, the novelist writes, "we go toward the core of the matter but never quite get to it"; for there is no "core" foreseeable or expected here, no deadline or "dénouement," and thus no desire to ride there hell for leather.

The Path-Novel

Banquet. Variations. To these two models—or countermodels—of novels written "in such a way that they cannot be retold" or summarized, another one can be added, and it is, once again, the "final walk" Agnès takes that afternoon—that is, barely a few hours before "Mr. Kundera" and Avenarius open their table talk about the art of the novel—along the mountain paths near the hotel where she spent the night. If, as we've seen, this walk and these paths offer the best image of the both diverse and unified semantic space that makes up the "massif" of Kundera's oeuvre and tells us the appropriate way for reading it, it is surely because they also provide one of the best metaphors for the way that space is constructed—that is, for Kundera's art of composition and for the ideal form he strives for, one of a novel which is not like "a narrow street along which someone drives his characters with a whip" but rather one of those winding, varied, really endless mountain paths that "branch into smaller paths, then into still smaller paths" to form a network the reader will enter as Agnès does: not to go somewhere, not to cover a distance, but, on the contrary, to stay there, to remain as long as possible within the boundless circle the novel traces and whose exploration can no more end for Agnès than knowledge of the forest in the midst of which she is taking her walk.

It's largely because it invented and made famous the art of the "path-novel" that the author of *The Art of the Novel* and *Testaments Betrayed* is so attached to what he calls the "first half" of the history of the novel. In Rabelais, in Cervantes, and later in Sterne, Fielding, or Diderot, the novel is not yet under the rule of the unity of action and dramatic tension, nor even under that of balanced and correct composition. By taking the form of wandering (*Don Quixote*), of a walk (*Jacques the Fatalist*), of uninhibited conversation (*The Decameron, Tristram Shandy*), it fears no sudden inspirations, bifurcations, distractions, episodes, indeed even discrepancies and inconclusive endings, instead seeking them out and not worrying over the problems such things could make for the order or the progress of the story. The intent of the novel here is not to move the reader logically, credibly, and effectively from one point to another. It consists rather in leading him astray, delaying him, or at least constantly drawing him away from his itinerary into what an enthusiast of walking of Goethe's day described as "a succession of tours and detours, of narrowings and broadenings"* where there are no more straight lines, no main nor secondary trails, because they all intertwine and run into each other so that the walker is never sure if he is going forward or retracing his steps and might at any moment find himself in a setting completely different from the one he had only just left.

That wish to revive "the superbly heterogeneous universe of those earliest novelists and . . . the liberty with which they dwelt in it" is one of the basic givens of Kundera's project as a novelist. And so we can say that, in a certain way, to read Kundera is to (re)learn to read the "earliest novelists," to (re)activate in us the frames of mind and aesthetic expectations that make us capable of entering their universe not as visitors to a superb, bygone moment of history but to be there freshly, immediately, fully at home. Not that the Kunderian novel is concerned with identically reproducing the methods of

---

*Karl Gottlob Schelle, *L'Art de se promener* (The Art of Walking), trans. Pierre Deshusses (1802; reprint: Paris, 1996), p. 91.

the old masters, as in "neo" art and other "revivals." In returning to Boccaccio, Rabelais, or Sterne, while it proceeds from nostalgic admiration and the desire to be faithful to the forgotten "testament" of these great precursors, it does not aim to regain this or that technique, this or that style, but rather to rediscover the novel's inherent freedom—that is, a form and spirit cleared of the constraints and conventions under which the novel's own successes, since the great Flaubert era, have come to crush and congeal it. What *Tristram Shandy* or *Jacques the Fatalist* bring to Kundera is the right to do what every novelist must do on his own: reinvent the art of the novel, discover new possibilities in it, and thus free it of its chains and of its automatic habits in order both to recall it to its basic vocation and to make it produce something new.

From the formal point of view, that is the primary ambition of what I call the path-novel. It's not a matter of rejecting the novelistic aesthetic of the novel inherited from the nineteenth century but rather—while keeping faith with the artistic and architectural concerns that are its most precious contribution—of breaking the mold; that is, of breaking free of the obligations and limitations that this aesthetic has come to impose: unity, verisimilitude, and continuous plot development based on causal and temporal linearity and on a strict ranking of the actions and the characters; homogeneity and sovereignty of the narration, which leads on the one hand to the disappearance of all other discourse—or at least to its relegation to a secondary level—and on the other to the obliteration or neutralization of the novelist's voice, reclothed as that of a mere "narrator"; finally, the documentary endeavor, by means of the faithful and detailed depiction of a "milieu" and a "moment"—that is, of a coherent and recognizable sociohistorical environment. In this sense Kundera's oeuvre really belongs—in the wake of those of the great immediate precursors it acknowledges: Kafka, Musil, Broch, Gombrowicz—to that "third (or overtime) period" of the novel's history, in which it takes note of the exhaustion of the realist canon and rediscovers the "unlimited liberty of formal invention" that brightened its pre-Balzac origins and opens itself to some formal potentialities of its own that had remained unexplored.

Among these potentialities is that of a novel that can reconcile "the easygoing freedom of Rabelais or Sterne . . . with the requirements of composition" (*Testaments Betrayed*), that is, a novel that would be *at the same time* as unfettered as possible and the most sturdily structured, the lightest and most dense, in which extreme diversity is wedded to a flawless unity, simplicity to complexity, the chanciness of *improvisation* to the necessities of *composition.* A novel, in short, in which the form resembles that of the "world of paths" in which Agnès's mind, on that afternoon, like that of Sterne's reader, "wanders off in sweet lazy liberty," given up to that "continuous and constantly changing" beauty which she is offered as she goes by, the endlessly different views of the selfsame mountain.

A Canon for Several Voices

Slowing the narrative flow; freeing the novel from the "narrow street" to which it has been confined; treating each fragment of its course as a moment of irreplaceable richness: in Kundera this project is achieved by combined recourse to two equally important principles of composition. The first is a principle of variety: it is *polyphony*, from which arises the "constantly changing" material of the novel. The second, on which its "continuity" rests, is *thematic unity.*

In music, the author of *The Art of the Novel* makes clear, polyphony is distinguished by "the *simultaneous* presentation of two or more voices." Transposed into the novel's domain, it therefore implies the rejection of "*unilinear* composition" in favor of a structure in which a multiplicity of lines meet and enter into a "contrapuntal" relation in which none can be called primary or secondary, subsidiary or dominant, but in which all enjoy the same status, the same relative autonomy, and are all equally necessary to one another and to the harmony and significance of the group.

The lines that make up the material of polyphonic composition can be of several kinds. The most obvious, because its material is closest to that of musical polyphony, is the doubling or multiplication of narrative "voices," a technique foreshadowed, for example, in the eighteenth-century epistolary novel, in the Balzac of *Mémoires de deux jeunes mariées* or, closer to our time, in the "Alexandria Quartet," which its author said he constructed as "a four-decker novel whose form is based on the relativity proposition"—that is, on the confrontation of the gazes leveled by four different minds on the common universe in which they are all evolving.

In *The Joke* too there are four points of view: Ludvik's, Helena's, Jaroslav's, Kostka's. But while Lawrence Durrell stays with the same narrator, Darley (except in *Mountolive*, which is written in the third person), and deals separately with each of the viewpoints, each of which he encloses, so to speak, in a separate book of his tetralogy, Kundera not only immediately gives a voice and the role of narrator to each member of his quartet (who in turn speaks in the first person) but also brings them together, beyond their respective monologues, within an ensemble where each one, while speaking for himself, is also unwittingly clarifying and completing his companions' remarks, a bit like what happens in that "canon for several voices" made up by the indistinct verses recited here and there in the Moravian village by the horsemen in the Ride of the Kings. Ludvik describes it as "a music sublime and *polyphonic*," where "each of the heralds declaimed in a monotone, on the same note throughout, but each on a different pitch, so that the voices combined unwittingly into a chord."

In *The Joke*'s structure, this polyphonic effect is initially obtained by the assignment to each of the four monologues of a style, a tone, and even of a content that is unique and that clearly sets it apart from the others, that is, of a "vocal autonomy" as great as possible. But at the same time none of the monologues (except Kostka's) unfolds all in one piece, in isolation from the others. Each of them, on the contrary, is cut up into a certain number of "interventions" of variable length, which allows each to be intertwined among the others, arranged so that the talk of each participant is constantly cut off, disrupted, given nuance, relativized by those of the others. Thus Ludvik speaks (and yields) twelve times, Helena four, and Jaroslav seven. Owing to this discontinuity, the four voices, while never "replying" directly (as in the epistolary novel), seem to be having an involuntary conversation and together actually forming a kind of narrative "canon." During the first six parts of the novel, the exchanges are still rather slow and the "replies" isolated from one another: heard in turn are Ludvik (nine pages), Helena (eleven), Ludvik again (eighty-nine), Jaroslav (thirty-nine), Ludvik once again (forty-one), and Kostka, at last (forty). But the tempo picks up in Part Seven (sixty-nine pages), in which the voices of Ludvik, Helena, and Jaroslav—no longer explicitly identified at each entry but always recognizable—follow one another so rapidly that they seem to be juxtaposed and singing from the same score.

Ludvik's monologue of course does have a more important position than the others, in quantitative as well as dramatic terms, because *The Joke* is above all (though not uniquely) his own story, the story of his fall and his revenge. But for all that the voices are still equal. Not only are Ludvik's utterances constantly interrupted (and thus cast into doubt) by those of the others, but with regard to himself and his destiny, with regard to the world in which he lives and has lived, with regard to Lucie, the silent young woman he used to love, nothing permits one to think that his vision would be better, more complete, or more right than that—equally sincere and equally partial—of Helena, Jaroslav, or Kostka. So that Ludvik's voice, no more than anyone else's, neither silences nor undercuts the voices of the others; neither he nor anyone here has the last word or the privilege of truth, if indeed the truth even exists apart from that multiplicity of voices and gazes turning toward it or, better, circling around it without ever possessing it.

It is one of the great constants of the Kunderian aesthetic—and irony—that this array of viewpoints on the same object which, being thus explained from contradictory angles, soon loses all unity and stability and starts wavering in its very identity and meaning. The "Third Day" of *Farewell Waltz*: is it advisable, yes or no, to have children? Act Four of "Symposium": did Elisabet try, yes or no, to kill herself? and why would she behave this way? As with Panurge's question in Rabelais's *Third Book*, there is no answer to these questions other than the debate they induce, which never settles them. For among all the "theories" Bertlef, Skreta, and Jakub advance in the first instance, and Flajsman, the chief physician, Havel, and the woman doctor in the second, the novel does not decide among them, so that none of them ends the uncertainty. Until the end the truth remains impossible to grasp or, rather, inseparable from the multiplicity of interpretations and words that all of them together can only pursue without ever grasping. Like the intertwining monologues of *The Joke*, dialogue here sets up a space around the question, in which all answers are deferred.*

In his *Système des beaux-arts*, the French thinker Alain, who was a great reader of the novelists of the "second half" (Balzac, Stendhal, Dickens, to whom he added Rousseau, whose *Confessions* he felt to be "the model of the novel") summarized thus what he considers a law of the "imagination proper to the novel": "In a novel there is always a center of perspective, in other words, a thinking principal subject, relative to whom the other characters have the role of objects"; "and, just as I am not two persons," he was careful to specify, "only one character of the kind is needed." With their multiple and changing "centers of perspective"—one might say, their centerless, fragmented perspective—*The Joke* and "Symposium" are in flagrant violation of this law of the "single-voice novel."

Also in violation, although in a somewhat different fashion, are the third and fifth stories in *Laughable Loves*, "The Hitchhiking Game" and "Let the Old Dead Make Room for the Young Dead," as is a novel like *Identity*, stories that no longer have a unique and constant "center of perspective" but whose entire arrangement, on

---

*On this subject see Jocelyn Maixent's fine essay "Vertus et vices de la parole romanesque: *Risibles Amours* ou les leçons de *Jacques*," *Dix-neuf vingt* (1996), as well as his book *Le XVIIIe siècle de Milan Kundera ou Diderot investi par le roman contemporain* (Paris 1998).

the contrary, illustrates exactly the absence—or the loss—of such a center. Although their narration is in the third person, these three stories rely, like *The Joke*, on the alternation between the visions—or the interior "voices"—of two characters. But while the voices of Ludvik and his fellow characters belong to people whom life has made more or less strangers to one another, the separate voices in *Identity* (or in these two stories from *Laughable Loves*) are those of two lovers. And during the story these voices not only differ one from the other and follow parallel lines, as do the monologues in *The Joke*: they also move off, get lost, are increasingly out of harmony. Chantal and Jean-Marc's drama, like that of the two young people in "The Hitchhiking Game," comes not only from their no longer managing to harmonize their voices or experiencing the things that happen to them in the same way. It is that they no longer know how to find their voices: the visions each has of the other and of himself are multiple, unstable, contradictory, and they no longer know where in all that confusion the truth is and where the error. Polyphony is their very intimacy and identity.

Intertwining Stories

In the preceding examples, the effect derives from the presence of several different viewpoints within the same story or the same fictional universe, whose unity is thereby diffracted into multiple interpretations, like a light source seen through a kaleidoscope. Equally interesting polyphonic possibilities can come from the interaction within the same story of two or several "lines" of separate *narrative* content; that is, lines made up of the adventures and thoughts of different characters or groups of characters and told simultaneously or in parallel. Thus, in *The Unbearable Lightness of Being*, Parts Two and Four, focused on Tereza, alternate with Parts One and Five, focused on Tomas, while the parts or pairs of parts focused on the couple Tereza-Tomas alternate with Parts Three and Six, focused on Sabina and Franz.

The intersection of stories is pushed still further in that veritable narrative ballet, *Farewell Waltz*. The Ruzena-Klima affair that serves as a release mechanism is soon joined by four or five other plots that in themselves have nothing to do with the first, and bring onstage characters who are total strangers there: Skreta, Jakub and Olga, Kamila, Frantisek. Although each of these stories follows its own course and obeys its own logic, the tale never ceases, chapter after chapter and even while respecting the linear unfolding of the five "Days," to jump from one to the other, from the actions of this character to the thoughts of that one, in a constantly oscillating movement at once perfectly free and perfectly regulated. Thus between each character's particular story and those of the others, all kinds of circumstantial connections and encounters are established that create an increasingly dense, soon inextricable network, in the midst of which coincidences, random occurrences, and "miracles" can multiply almost infinitely. Of none of these stories, however, can one say that it constitutes the *main* action of the novel, any more than any of the characters in it stands as its *hero*. Between the stories as between the characters reign, according to the author of *The Art of the Novel,* "the conditions *sine qua non* for counterpoint in the novel . . . first, the equality of the various 'lines,' and second, the indivisibility of the whole."

These are the same conditions that govern the narrative architecture of Kundera's third French novel, *Ignorance,* whose plot (return to the homeland) is linked, as I've already noted, with that of *Farewell Waltz* (departure from it). In fifty-three brief chapters, *Ignorance* tells the stories of three apparently unconnected characters. For the first eleven chapters, the action is focused on Irena, a Czech émigré living in Paris whom the collapse of Communism induces to return to Prague, where she has not set foot for twenty years. At the airport Irena by chance comes across a man she seems to recognize, Josef. Then the story suddenly branches off, and the chapters that follow are entirely devoted to Josef's story; he too is an émi-gré returning to Bohemia to see his family and friends again. The reader must wait until Chapter 25 for the reappearance of Irena, who for some pages temporarily regains the role of protagonist. Then, in Chapters 28 and 29, another branching: a third story takes form, that of an unnamed girl who emerges out of an old diary from Josef's youth; only at the end do we learn that this girl is Milada, one of the friends Irena has just rediscovered. From this point on the three stories are told in increasingly rapid alternation, as if, after having followed Irena's "path" for some time, and then Josef's, we are entering a part of the forest where the paths multiply and shorten, and form an increasingly dense, indivisible labyrinth, in which the stories are only a single plural story, off center and yet coherent, that in the ten last chapters culminates in a kind of parallel montage like the one that ends the "Fourth Day" of *Farewell Waltz*.

One last illustration, perhaps the most magnificent, of such polyphonic narration would be Part Five of *Immortality*, whose construction has a vertiginous quality about it. The central structure alternates two different stories that unfold on the same day, from lunchtime until about the beginning of the night. One, which is set in motion in the first three chapters, recounts Agnès's final afternoon in Switzerland, her journey by car toward

Paris, her accident, and finally her death, alone, in a provincial hospital. The other, which begins in Chapter 4, takes place in Paris; it brings onstage "Mr. Kundera" and his friend Professor Avenarius; they converse on various subjects, first at a swimming pool, then in a restaurant, and finally in the street, where the two men separate. Avenarius then embarks on another of his nocturnal operations against "Diabolum," but this time he is arrested.

The two stories thus do not at all have the same status, and we might say that the first is embedded in the second, seeing that Agnès, as we know from the very first pages of the novel, is a character imagined by "Mr. Kundera," who, moreover, discusses her with Avenarius during their lunch in the restaurant. This dichotomy does not at all prevent the two stories, at the end of this Part Five, when both are marked by cries of terror ripping through the night, from coming together in one: Avenarius's arrest in fact takes place on the street where Paul, Agnès's husband, lives and, in his capacity as a lawyer, goes to the professor's aid, before rushing off to the provincial city where, he has just learned, his wife is hovering between life and death. So where, in which world, does Avenarius move, he who on the one hand can converse with the author of the novel and on the other encounter its characters? Where is the "real"; where does "fiction" begin?

But that's not all. Here comes a third story intruding between the two others and weaving between them an additional bond: that of the suicidal girl. This unnamed character appears in Chapter 9, as an entirely hypothetical creature arising from a radio news item "Mr. Kundera" mentions during his conversation with Avenarius. By being imagined, dreamed up by the novelist and his friend, the girl little by little takes on substance and soon becomes as "real" as Agnès or Paul, so much so that her story pulls away from the conversation with Avenarius, as it were takes on autonomy, and in Chapters 15 and 17 ends up the object of a purely "objective" tale, in which the girl's acts and thoughts cause Agnès's fatal accident.

While they are not totally devoid of a certain playful dimension, it's obvious that such feats of narrative intertwinement have primarily a semantic or cognitive function that they alone are able to fulfill. Thus the invention of the suicidal-girl story in this part of *Immortality*, by the counterpoint it establishes with that of Agnès, casts a distinctive light on Agnès and on her death. The two women certainly feel the desire to escape from the "painful self" (the girl), from the "hurting self" (Agnès), but their desire is not exactly the same: while the one wants to die because she feels her soul rejected and humiliated in the world, the other seeks only "to escape, to escape forever" a world and a soul that have become alien to her. But the border between the two desires remains extremely thin, and the juxtaposition of the two characters opens a question that is the mystery of Agnès herself: how far does her need to disappear go? how can she still live when everything pushes her toward "a world without faces"? what keeps her, in short, from taking her life as the girl wants to do? For at no moment does Agnès wish to die. But chance (which gives this Part Five its title) decides otherwise: the threads of the two stories get tangled, the two characters exchange destinies, and Agnès dies while the suicidal girl continues to live. Such chance is all the more ironic—and all the more beautiful—since it is in fact a matter of doubled chance: the effect of a highly improbable coincidence between her own movements and those of an unknown girl, Agnès's death is at the same time only a rather secondary circumstance in a story engendered, some hundreds of kilometers away, by the table talk of two cheerful companions.

As this example already shows, the encounter—by alternation and embedding—of multiple stories inside the same space in the novel is all the more striking as these stories do not occupy exactly the same levels of reality (or of fiction). If it can be said, for example, that all the characters in *The Joke* or in *Farewell Waltz* live at the same time in the same universe and possess the same ontological status, that is no longer true in Part Five of *Immortality*, where the universe of "Mr. Kundera" and his friend is in principle separate from the one in which, on the one hand, Agnès and Paul, and on the other, the suicidal girl, are active.

But the disparity of the universes susceptible to being thus summoned and melded in the novel's polyphonic crucible is still greater. Beside or inside the fictional world where the characters' stories unfold, a good many other worlds can open and maintain a variety of connections with it. Three examples come to mind: the world of dreams, the world of the past, and the world of the novelist.

Stories Dreamed

Dreams are frequent in Kundera's oeuvre, and they are distinguished by two features. First, they are rarely mere visions but nearly always adventures; that is, *tales* in which all the usual ingredients of narration are to be found—sequential action, settings, characters, and even dialogues. Certainly these characters, these settings, these plots, as well as the temporality and the causality that structure them, have little to do with the conventions of ordinary verisimilitude, but the manner of their exposition remains very near to that which governs the narration of stories that we might call "real," that is, those that unfold in the primary fictional world. This formal attribute is precisely what allows these dreams, despite their belonging to a different order of verisimilitude, to enter the polyphonic composition of the novel on an equal footing together with the other narrative "lines."

Together with and *equal* to them. Because—and this is the second feature—no matter how much the dreams bring up a world other than that of the "ordinary" reality in which the characters move—or how much they derive from that strangeness some essential part of their power of fascination—in Kundera's novels this other world never seems either more or less real, or more or less meaningful, than the first. Instead of the customary literary uses for dreamlike tales—a prophetic or "psychoanalytic" use on the one hand, an ornamental one on the other—the Kunderian novel substitutes a purely aesthetic treatment: it is attached to the dream's content not as to the cause or the effect or the sign of something else, but for its own sake and for its own enigmatic beauty, taking care not to subordinate it somehow to the principal narrative or to any other element of the composition. Dreams thereby acquire a presence that is fully equal to that of the "real" stories, and their role in depicting the characters and in examining meanings is as decisive as the role of any other component of the novel, or as any other of the multiple "paths" that run through it.

This equality of two ontological areas—dream and "reality"—permits diverse kinds of relations between them, from their sharp separation to forms of reconciliation that make them practically indistinguishable from each other. The first case is illustrated in *The Unbearable Lightness of Being* by Tereza's serial dreams, which tell a second story alongside that of her liaison with Tomas—an internal, strange story whose main themes do reverberate in the first story, but without the two worlds merging in the narration, and with the reader always knowing in which of the two he finds himself. Elsewhere the distinction only arises after a fairly long moment of hesitation. Initially we enter a story whose rules or setting introduce an unusual, uncertain quality, to discover later that it's a dream story out of some character's imagination. That is what happens at the beginning of Part Four of *The Joke*, when Jaroslav appears for the first time as a character in a tale (we discover in the following chapter) that he is dreaming.

The same thing happens, in a still more striking way, in *Life Is Elsewhere*, when, in Part Two, the strange adventures of the character named Xavier are introduced as a kind of independent novel, half slapstick, half spy movie, stuck into the "realistic" novel about

Jaromil and lacking any visible connection with it. There again it is only later, even much later, that their true nature and origins are revealed: it is made clear in Part Five of the novel that Jaromil had "dreamed [Xavier's] adventures and wanted to write them down someday." This reduction, this dissolution, of Xavier's story and world, suddenly returned to their dream status and retrieved, so to speak, into Jaromil's story and world, nevertheless doesn't prevent Xavier from continuing his novelistic existence in the young poet's consciousness until the two figures end up merging into each other shortly before Jaromil's death:

> In the beginning there was only Jaromil.
>
> Then Jaromil created Xavier, his double, and with him his other life, dreamlike and adventurous.
>
> And now the moment has come to end the contradiction between dream and waking, between poetry and life, between action and thought. At the same time the contradiction between Xavier and Jaromil has also vanished.

Virtually copied from André Breton's Second *Manifesto of Surrealism*,* the paragraph above can be read

---

* "Everything tends to make us believe that there exists a certain point of the mind at which life and death, the real and the imagined, past and future, the communicable and the incommunicable, high and low, cease to be perceived as contradictions." (André Breton, *Manifestoes of Surrealism*, trans. Richard Seaver and Helen R. Lane [Ann Arbor, Mich., 1972], p. 123.)

ironically: the gap between dream and reality may well disappear for Jaromil, but this gap still persists in the reader's mind; or if it also disappears there, that is not because the two worlds have miraculously fused but because "Xavier" has truly ceased to exist. As thrilling and beautiful as it is, the dream he lived in is now merely one of the "lives elsewhere," merely one of the illusions behind which the infatuated Jaromil's innocence takes shelter.

If dreamlike narratives, in the examples above, constitute a separate world with relatively precise limits, there are other cases in which these limits tend to dissolve and allow the substance and the strangeness of dream to leak into the world of the "real," giving rise to composite stories in which one cannot tell where—in which universe—they actually unfold. Such is the case in *The Book of Laughter and Forgetting*, with Tamina's stay on the children's island that is the subject of Part Six, which ends with the heroine's disappearance. The episode begins like a "normal" story: in the café in the small Western European town where she works as a waitress, Tamina is visited by a "young fellow in jeans" who seems like any other customer and says things to her that she at first doesn't see as unusual. Soon, though, the young man with an archangel's name—Raphael—a name that arouses suspicion because it is that of the French teacher in Part Three of the novel—induces Tamina to get into his car and takes her far away from the town. The story then tilts imperceptibly, and a new world and a new logic take over that have nothing to do with what had been Tamina's life till then. She finds herself on a mysterious island entirely populated by children, among whom she is at once queen and prisoner, a new Gulliver in the land of Lilliput, a new Gregor Samsa suddenly stripped of ordinary reference points and condemned to struggle with the improbable. Very quickly her distress becomes intolerable, and Tamina ends up throwing herself into the water, hoping to reach the mainland. But the mainland is no more, "reality" is no more, and the nightmare closes over her and carries her off. We have subtly been moved from the café in the provincial town to a universe of pure fantasy all the more troubling in that it is impossible to know for sure if this is, in the novel's words, a "dream" or a "tale"—that is, a hallucination of Tamina's or a metaphorical depiction of her death, she who has already once attempted suicide by drowning. Nor can we understand whether Tamina "really" dies, and how. All that's certain is that a border has been crossed, or obliterated, and that we have been covertly made to slip from one world into another. But which of the two is the real world, Tamina's world?

In his first two French novels, so realistic in certain aspects, Kundera again plays on that ambiguity with obvious pleasure. A bit like Part Six of *The Book of Laughter and Forgetting*, the final chapters of *Identity* in turn describe a journey through spaces that are half familiar (a railroad station, the Channel Tunnel, England), half eerie ("Britannicus's" house, a broom closet, doors nailed shut, and the like) where the demarcation is vague to begin with and becomes more so. Because once we have entered Chantal and Jean-Marc's nightmare, even our initial sense of their reality becomes problematic. Along with the novelist, we ask ourselves:

> Who dreamed this story? Who imagined it? She? He? Both of them? Each one for the other? And starting when did their real life change into this treacherous fantasy? . . . At what exact moment did the real turn into the unreal, reality into reverie? Where was the border? Where is the border?

Is there even a border? In any case, *Identity* knows none; it allows the two levels to interpenetrate freely and thereby becomes perhaps the most Kafkan of Kundera's novels, if one agrees, with the author of *The Art of the Novel* to define the "enormous aesthetic revolution" Kafka carried out as the invention of a narrative mode "in which dream and reality are bound together, so fully mingled that one cannot be distinguished from the other."

Without turning into the nightmare into which the lovers in *Identity* are hurled, the fusion of worlds is also the structural principle of *Slowness*. The basic reality, the initial fictional universe here, is reduced to a minimum: the novelist and his wife, Véra, dine and spend the night at a château-hotel in the French countryside. The whole novel "embedded" in this story (or this nonstory) is structured as a counterpoint binding (and opposing) two dreams come to haunt this old residence and to populate this enchanted night. One, the "present-day" story, introduces Vincent and his companions and is so noisy that twice it wakes Véra, while the other, a re-creation of *Point de lendemain*, an eighteenth-century novella by Vivant Denon, is all silence, sensual pleasure, and slowness. In the morning the three worlds—the novelist and Véra in their car, Vincent on his motorcycle, the Chevalier in his carriage—briefly intersect in the château-hotel's parking lot, where they mysteriously exchange their realities as well as their unrealities before each vanishes in its own direction.

Stories from the Past

If, to some degree, it belongs to the realm of dream, the *Slowness* story inspired by *Point de lendemain* draws on a third ontological terrain to which Kunderian art grants preferential rank as well: the past—that is, the characters and the events from European history that can, as naturally as those from the underlying fictional universe or as the oneiric figures and stories, constitute another of the "lines" upon which the polyphonic syntax of the novel is structured.

The most striking illustration of this process is of course to be found in *Immortality*, in which Parts Two and Four insert into the midst of the novel of Agnès and her family, which unfolds in twentieth-century France, a long account set in nineteenth-century Germany and presenting Goethe, his wife Christiane, his admirer Bettina Brentano, and some of their contemporaries, among them Beethoven. Motivated by the affection for Goethe's poetry that Agnès inherited from her father, this sudden jump not only takes us from one era to another but also, more radically, from the world of fiction (Agnès's life) to that of historical reality. This account of the relationship between Goethe and Bettina has nothing to do with the more or less bastard genre of romanticized history or biography à la Scott or Dumas, not to speak of many other more recent examples. On the contrary, the facts here are reported with the greatest possible accuracy and rigor: they are dated and detailed, and their documentary basis (Goethe and Bettina's writings) is cited and examined critically as well as in the diverse versions that have been put forward by the interpretive tradition (Rilke, Romain Rolland, Eluard). If it were not an artifact of novelistic play, the only things the story analysis would lack to meet all the method's requirements are footnotes and a bibliography. It does lack something else as well, of course, and that is the main thing: the goal of this reconstruction of an episode from the past, and of the research that preceded it, is definitely not to know or explain that past as past. Their function is far different; it is essentially, uniquely *novelistic*: to cut across the forest of the oeuvre another path around its meaning, which is all that matters. That is why the "historical" story, any more than the dream story, cannot be isolated from the other components of the novel with which it enters into relationships. And so, in *Immortality*, the Goethe and Agnès stories, both of them traversed by characters (Bettina-Laura), by gestures (the gesture of the longing for immortality), by situations (the broken eyeglasses) that seem to replicate each other, create a single meditation in two inseparable panels, the one—fictional—located in a time and an existence that resemble our own, the other—historical—located in the distant, detemporalized space that is the world of the dead, the world of the immortals.

In *Life Is Elsewhere* a similar "polytemporal" structure is provided by the presence around Jaromil of all those figures of renowned poets whose stories constantly accompany his own as glorious shadows or echoes from the past, a past so alive and so nearby that, by Part Seven of the novel, the poets and Jaromil form a single being with a thousand interchangeable faces, a single Poet over whom neither time nor place has control. Jaromil becomes Lermontov, and Lermontov becomes Jaromil. For if it's true that Lermontov, Rimbaud, Mayakovsky, Breton, and the others add to our understanding of Jaromil, the reverse is also true: the Jaromil hypothesis, that is, the fictional existence of this character placed in a specific historical context, in return casts a new light on the known existence of Rimbaud, Lermontov, Mayakovsky, Breton, and the others—that is, on the "existential mathematics" of modern lyricism—discovering in it aspects that would otherwise be impossible to perceive.

"History," Tocqueville says, "is like a picture gallery in which there are few originals and many copies." And Kundera, in *Testaments Betrayed*, says of Thomas Mann's oeuvre: "We think we act, we think we think, but it is another or others who think and act in us: that is to say, timeless habits, archetypes, which—having become myths passed on from one generation to the next—carry an enormous seductive power and control us (says Mann) from 'the well of the past.'" Far from obeying some historicist vision, the novelistic use of the past is therefore equivalent, paradoxically, if not to a negation of history and its determinations, then at least to the—hypothetical—statement of an "existential law" more significant than any progress or any particular context to which it is "applicable." Bettina's Germany certainly does continue to "act" and to "think" in Laura's contemporary France, just as Lermontov's existence is extended—and repeated—in Jaromil's. The bygone world is just as present as the world of today, if not even more present and more "real," insofar as the passage of time and the fact of death give it the purity and the exemplary quality of a paradigm: its successors' gestures are then just permutations, new variations that repeat and modulate a theme already determined even before their own adventure begins. Memory and mirror, the past thus creates an ironic and hermeneutic rim around the present that both makes it ordinary and illuminates it.

As I've already noted, the same type of temporal counterpoint can be found in *Slowness*, where the erotic nights of Vincent and of Vivant Denon's Chevalier echo one another over an interval of two centuries. But this case is somewhat different from those of *Immortality* and *Life Is Elsewhere*. First, *Slowness*'s characters and facts from the past do not belong to actual history but to literary fiction, and this gives them a fragility, an ontological evanescence that the "real" characters Goethe or

Lermontov don't have. Second, the connection between the two worlds no longer rests on their resemblance to each other but on what sets them symmetrically opposite to each other; this time, temporal distance stands as an impassable barrier between Vincent and the Chevalier. Finally—and this point is crucial—the past that is evoked refers not to the nineteenth or the early twentieth century, as in *Life Is Elsewhere* or *Immortality*, but to the eighteenth century of the libertines—that is, to an infinitely distant, vanished era with which all continuity seems to be definitively broken.

If one actually attempts, using the images of the past that run through Kundera's novels, to derive the general vision that inspires them, it would be that of a European history divided into two great eras or two entirely different anthropological ages, whose break would correspond roughly to the one that divides into the two "half-times" of the history of the novel as described by the author of *Testaments Betrayed*. Between the two, at the exact point of their demarcation, that is, "precisely in the center of European history" stands Goethe, "the great center" where the earlier age closes while the one we live in opens.

Only the first of these two ages is properly speaking the *past*. It corresponds to the pre-Romantic, pre-Hegelian world that goes from the Renaissance to the

French Revolution and that the figure of Don Juan embodies par excellence; but its territory extends much further still, past history in fact, back to the original homeland of the great founding myths: Oedipus (*The Unbearable Lightness of Being*), Odysseus (*Ignorance*), Daphnis and Chloe (*The Book of Laughter and Forgetting*), Herod and Jesus (*Farewell Waltz*), the homeland too of that "ancient world" recalled in *The Joke* by Jaroslav's beloved Moravian songs and by the mysterious ritual of the Ride of the Kings. But about this past, "no one [any longer] knows what it means, what it wants to say," because it reaches us only as vague echoes, like the fossil radiation that astronomers study at the edge of the universe for an image of its initial splendor. So we can only connect with this drowned continent, this homeland forever lost, through a "great yearning" like Jan's for Daphnis, and the ironic awareness of being forever exiled from it. If this past continues to "remote control" our present and that of the characters, it does serve above all to show the present as the location, if not of its disappearance then at least of its irremediable erosion, where there remain only diminished images—imitations, parodies, jokes—all the more ridiculous in that both their source and our insuperable distance from it are forgotten. And so Vincent and Julie's night unfolds as an unintended and grotesque pastiche of the sublime night of the Cheva-

lier and Madame de T. And it is also against the "historical background" in which Don Juan evolved that Dr.
Havel can understand the "comic sadness of [his] wom-
anizing existence." In short, between that distant past
and the present, the counterpoint necessarily takes the
form of an antithesis.

This is no longer the case when we get to the second
age of the Kunderian vision of history, since that age,
which rises on the ruins or the forgetting of the first, in
fact corresponds to *our* world, the world of revolution
and progress, of internal mediation and of the triumphal
self, a world to which belong (and that suits) Bettina as
well as Laura, Lermontov as well as Jaromil. It can be
said that if the Chevalier and Madame de T. are certainly,
among the characters gathered at *Slowness*'s château-
hotel, truly visitors come from an "alien" time, that is not
so of Lermontov, Rimbaud, and Bettina, who in stepping
from the nineteenth century to the world of the present,
in reality are only moving within a time that remains basically the same. That is why, in *Immortality*'s heaven,
Goethe and Hemingway can speak the same language.
And it is also why, in *Life Is Elsewhere*, the Czechoslovakia of the years 1930–50 during which the fictional
existence of Jaromil unfolds is in keeping not only with
the previous century but also with the *future*, especially
when the events of May 1968 are recalled. These three

moments—the past of the great lyric poets, the present of Jaromil, the future of the Paris students—are actually a single era, a single space with many connecting rooms in which recur the same dreams, the same gestures, the same romantic need for constant change, for excess, and for rebellion—that is, for an ending. Going from Laura to Bettina, from Jaromil to Mayakovsky, is thus for the novel merely a way of seeking everywhere its sole treasure: the concrete existence of modern man in "the trap the world has become" amid ambushes and other decoys set for him by his desires large and small, his loves, his hatreds, his irrepressible need for consolation and salvation—that is, his incapacity to be only what he is.

This is why any reading that sees Kundera's novels primarily as documents of historical or sociological interest, as a certain kind of criticism fascinated by the author's origins and personal destiny tends to do, can only be reductive and wrong. Admittedly, no survey, no work of history or political science "conveys" more precisely and as concretely the destiny of Czechoslovakia (and of Communist Europe) in the second half of the twentieth century than the five-panel tableau—consisting of *Life Is Elsewhere*, *The Joke*, *The Unbearable Lightness of Being*, *The Book of Laughter and Forgetting*, and *Ignorance*—which lays out the successive phases of a history that runs from World War II until the return of the émigrés. In recent novels there scarcely exists a depiction at once more fierce, more comic and thus more exact of the Western society known as "postmodern" than the triptych of "immediate history" made up of *Immortality*, *Slowness*, and *Identity*. But that kind of reading, which so delights journalists and professors, is doubly unfaithful to the novels it claims to decode: first of all it adds to them elements that are not there (notably dates, places, and names that the novelist has deliberately left vague); and above all it forces them away from their intention, which is not in the least to recount the history of a society or a regime but rather to recount human existence through certain situations exemplified by this society or that regime (like the complicity between poet and hangman in post-1948 Prague, or the terror wielded by the public gaze in the Europe of imagologists and "dancers"). No matter how much the country, the climate, the "historic" events, large and small, amid which the lives of Jaromil, of Tomas and Tereza, or of Vincent and Julie unfold may resemble reality, strictly speaking they are still only a circumstance, incidentals, a theater, and never the central subject of the picture. They play the role of existential catalyst, like romantic Germany in *Immortality* or the Nazi camp in *The Unbearable Lightness of Being*, where Yakov Stalin "laid down his life for shit." "To hell with portraying an era!" exclaims the author of *Life Is Elsewhere*. "What interests me is a young man who writes poems!" Who writes them, has written them, and will go on writing them forever.

The Novelist Self

The distinctive feature of novelistic polyphony is to create coexistence, not only of a multiplicity of independent voices, stories, and characters possessing the same fictional status but also of "lines" or *heterogeneous* layers of reality—and to do so without organizing them into a hierarchy or granting any one of them preeminence (as, for example, in *Life Is Elsewhere*, the worlds of Jaromil, Xavier, and Rimbaud). To these three worlds, to these three story reservoirs—"basic fiction," dream, the past—another can be added whose ontological heterogeneity is still greater since it is, strictly speaking, no longer from the realm of the imagined but from the realm of "real presence," and since it is no longer presenting invented or distant beings but rather the being who is nearest and most irrefutable of all: the novelist himself.

It is actually another feature of the Kunderian novel, what I would call the nonobliteration of the author and his assertion in the very midst of the narration through a clearly identified voice and thought that fear neither to indicate their presence nor to declare their position concerning the depicted universe, yet not removing its autonomy or its own reality. This feature, which is one way of reviving the orality of the "first half" novel and, in doing so, breaking the modern taboo that forbids the novelist to appear in person in the world of his characters, undergoes various transformations along the oeuvre. In *The Joke* and in the first two stories in *Laughable Loves*, the author's "I" has almost no room, since these three works—the only ones Kundera has written utilizing conventional first-person narration—are fairly permeated, as it were, by the fictional "I" of the characters, who are also its narrators. Yet the position of the one who speaks as "I" in "The Golden Apple of Eternal Desire" is not entirely that of a protagonist, as is the case in "Nobody Will Laugh" and in the monologues in *The Joke*, but nearly that of the author or at least of the both detached and tender observer of the adventures of the actual character, who is Martin. Perhaps Kundera abandoned this kind of narration because he quickly perceived its limitations: under cover of breaking with the artifice of omniscience, use of the first person only makes for a still more servile obedience to the dictate of the realist illusion and constrains still more the novelist's freedom.

Still, from the beginning of *Life Is Elsewhere*, as in

the five last stories of *Laughable Loves*, all the characters' tales are narrated in the good old third person. This
"regression" does not mean, however, that the author—
in his adoption of some "God's-eye view"—seeks to
hide behind his creatures or that he wants to make us
believe in some "impassivity" on his part. On the contrary, recourse to the "he" is exactly what allows the
novelist to free the grammatical first person for his own
use and to appear in his own novel.

These appearances initially remain discreet. In
Farewell Waltz, for example, there are only three of them,
rather late in the novel and each time in parentheses. The
same discretion is observable in the central stories of
Laughable Loves. In "Eduard and God," however, the
interventions become much more numerous. From the first
words ("Let me begin Eduard's story in his older brother's
little house in the country"), and regularly afterward, the
novelist's voice, sometimes conjugated as "we," sometimes
as "I," is addressed directly to "ladies and gentlemen"
readers, which is what gives this story its unserious, slightly
Boccaccian air of a tale told aloud by a storyteller to a
complicit and amused audience.

This procedure, whose principal effect is to defuse the
pretense of reality by stressing the fictional or "discursive" nature of the depicted events and characters, and
thus to bring out the playfulness of the oeuvre, is just as

pronounced in *Life Is Elsewhere*, where, however, it is given certain particular values. Instead of keeping to the detached position of a witness simply reporting the facts and accompanying the characters at a respectful distance, here the "we" narrator adopts a much less reserved attitude and starts to intervene *on his own account* in the course of the story. These interventions sometimes lead him to contest or rectify a character's view ("but we need to correct Mama's opinion on this point"), sometimes to add to his subject considerations the latter cannot know. For example, when a woman friend of the painter's shows interest in Jaromil, who reminds her, she says, "of Rimbaud with Verlaine and his friends in the painting by Fantin-Latour," a parenthesis opens:

> (I can't resist observing that this woman leaned over Jaromil with the same cruel tenderness as when the sisters of Rimbaud's teacher Izambard, the famous *"lice hunters,"* leaned over Rimbaud upon his return from one of his extended adventures and washed, cleaned, and deloused him.)

It's as if the novelist were throwing off the task of being a mere narrator and becoming, for a while, a separate and autonomous participant in the story. Becoming that, or rather abandoning the pretense of not being that, and ceasing to feign a distance and a neutrality that only hide the effective authority he exercises over his novel. Speaking up to explain his narrative decisions and say, for example: "Let's stop at this word . . . ," or, "I've chosen this episode among dozens of others in order to show that . . . ," he reveals at once that authority as well as the entirely relative nature of his powers. The finest example of this type of intervention is at the beginning of Part Six, where Jaromil's "biography" breaks off abruptly and a wholly new character, unknown to both the young poet and the reader, unexpectedly appears: the man in his forties. The novelist goes on to speak at length, disclosing his vantage point and his strategies regarding the work he is writing:

> The first part of this novel encompasses fifteen years of Jaromil's life, but the fifth part, which is longer, covers barely a year. . . . The reason for this is that we're looking at Jaromil from an observatory I've erected at the point of his death. . . . What if I swiftly and secretly dismantled my observatory and transported it elsewhere, if only temporarily? . . . Yes, let's leave this novel for a while, let's transport the observatory beyond Jaromil's life, and let's place it in the mind of an entirely different character made of completely different stuff. . . . Let's construct a part of the novel that will be related to all its other parts as the cottage on an estate is related to the mansion. . . . This sixth part of the novel, which I've compared to a cottage, takes place in a studio apartment. . . .

Another step toward the novelist's textual emancipation is taken in *The Book of Laughter and Forgetting*, which in this respect is a transitional work. The first point to emphasize about this: the abandonment of the anonymous "we," which retains something of the imprecise, in favor of a more personal and more concrete "I." The second point: The "I" is identified by name with the person of the author, "Mr. Kundera," who, as we've seen, will reappear under the same name in *Immortality* and under that of "Milanku" in *Slowness*.

There's more. In *The Book of Laughter and Forgetting*, the "I" itself sometimes becomes the central character of the novel. This occurs in Parts Three and Six (both titled "The Angels"), in which he recalls three carefully dated events whose narration mingles with Gabrielle and Michelle's summer studies and then with Tamina's stay on the children's island: (1) expulsion from the Communist Party in 1948–1950; (2) the era, "soon after the Russians occupied my country in 1968," "those years of exclusion [when I] cast thousands of horoscopes"; and (3) the encounter, in 1971, with the historian Hübl, followed, six months later, by the silent dying and death of "Papa." In the same vein is the passage in Part Five in which the novelist recalls the precise situation when he was writing this book:

It is the autumn of 1977, my country has been sweetly dozing for nine years now in the strong embrace of the Russian empire, . . . and my books, having been gathered up from all the public libraries, are locked away in some state cellar. I waited for a few years, and then I got into a car and drove as far west as possible, to the Breton town of Rennes, where on the first day I found an apartment on the top floor of the tallest high-rise tower. When the sun woke me the next morning, I realized its large windows faced east, toward Prague.

These pages show all the signs of an autobiographical account, beginning with the name shared among author, narrator, and character. But whatever their rhetorical appearance, these accounts, in fact, lack the essentials of the autobiographical *intention*, which is only achieved, says the genre's theoretician, when the author's "focus is his individual life, in particular the story of his personality,"* that is, to talk like Banaka, with his master's degree in graphomania, of his "experience *inside*" unlike anyone else's. Such is not at all the reason behind the stories about his past that the novelist puts into *The Book of Laughter and Forgetting* and that make up one "variation" *among others* in its composi-

*Philippe Lejeune, *On Autobiography*, trans. Katherine Leary (Minneapolis, 1989), p. 4.

tion. Their function is not to illustrate the singularity of his being, or "to report on his life," as Bibi so much wants to do, but, by the same token as the other fictional or real stories contained in the novel—those of Mirek, Mama, Jan and Edwige, and Tamina in particular, but also those of Eluard and of Clementis's hat—to contribute to exploring the themes that attract him: "looking back," laughter, angels. In other words the *self* that tells its tale here does so not as a lyrical subject fascinated by the uniqueness of its being and desirous of knowing itself and becoming known through gazing at itself in the confessional that is autobiography, or even "autofiction," but rather as a novelist self—that is, as construction foreman and participant in the novel being built. No matter that he calls that self "Mr. Kundera," no matter that he lived in Prague and moved to France around 1975, it is still a self that has no referent outside the novel in which it occurs. Its only existence is there; there all its adventures take place.

"Construction foreman," I've said. The "meddlings" of the novelist are so frequent and so developed in *The Book of Laughter and Forgetting* because the structure of this novel displays a particularly high degree of heterogeneity, since all its parts—except Four and Six—make up many autonomous stories, complete in themselves, each with its own characters and with no chronological or causal connections. So one of the functions of the "I" is to create, within this apparent disparity, some "vocal" permanence or continuity that points out the unity of the whole. From which, perhaps, one might state this rule: the more a novel's structure is splintered and its materials varied, the more the novelist's self shows. That presence will again be very pronounced in *The Unbearable Lightness of Being* and, even more, in *Immortality*, novels in which the dramatic continuity is often discontinuous, if not spotty, and where as a consequence the "I" intervenes from the opening pages: "Not long ago, I caught myself experiencing a most incredible sensation . . ."; "The woman might have been sixty or sixty-five. I was watching her from a deck chair." It occurs again in *Slowness*, where the novelist identifies himself right at the outset: "I am driving, and in the rearview mirror I notice a car behind me." On the other hand he is practically mute in *Identity*, in which narrative continuity and plot compression predominate.

Even in this latter novel, however, the "I" cannot restrain itself from appearing, at least covertly, at the very end: "I see their two heads, in profile, lit by the light of a little bedside lamp." Already utilized incidentally in *Life Is Elsewhere*, this self-introduction of the novelist as if he himself were present with his characters and lived in the same world with them is another peculiarity of the Kunderian novel. It occurs again in *Slowness*, for instance, when the novelist casually recalls his encounter with Goujard, one of Pontevin's pals, or when he contemplates Julie's naked body before putting "a question directly to Vincent's member"; or again, in the room where Véra is sleeping, when he sees through the window "two people strolling in the château's park by the light of the moon." Who are these two "people," or these "characters"? Julie and Vincent, who are just coming back from a stroll? Or perhaps the Chevalier and Madame de T., whose "unforgettable excursion" among the garden paths the novelist imagined as he opened the window a bit earlier the same night? But the finest of these encounters between the novelist and his imaginary creations is probably the one, already mentioned, that takes place in *Immortality*, when "Mr. Kundera" converses with Avenarius, himself an intimate of Laura's, and when the latter and her new husband, Paul, come at the end to join Avenarius and the novelist as he celebrates the completion of "my novel."

These contacts, these kinds of ontological transfers by which the novelist and his characters exchange their "reality" (or their "fictivity") are all the more gripping—and paradoxical—in that the imaginary nature of the characters has been strongly emphasized from the start, as happens again, in *The Book of Laughter and Forgetting*, when the character Tamina first appears:

> This time, to make clear that my heroine is mine and only mine (I am more attached to her than to any other), I am giving her a name no woman has ever before borne: Tamina. I imagine her as tall and beautiful, thirty-three years old, and originally from Prague.
>
> I see her walking down a street in a provincial town in the west of Europe.

Also to be born under the reader's eyes are the character Tomas, at the beginning of *The Unbearable Lightness of Being*: "I have been thinking about Tomas for many years. But only in the light of these reflections did I see him clearly"; and the character Agnès, in the second chapter of *Immortality*: "When I wake up, at almost eight-thirty, I try to picture Agnès. . . . For the first time I see her naked: Agnès, the heroine of my novel."

Thus no confusion is possible, nor any trickery as to what Sartre called the "freedom" of the character. Tamina is "mine," the novelist declares, meaning that she is of me, but also that she is not I. Something of me is in her (one of "my own unrealized possibilities"), but I am not hiding myself behind her completely; confronting her identity as a character I keep my own identity and elbow room as a novelist. In short, we stand one facing the other or each in the company of the other, in this novel that encompasses us both. And in which we will be two voices, two thoughts, two equal and inseparable existences seeking the same meaning.

The Novel's Thought

While it allows the dissipation or the attenuation of realist illusion, emancipation of the "novelist's self" also provides a space within the novel where the story is suspended and a new "line" in the novelistic polyphony can come into play: the essay—that is, a reflective or analytic discourse that directly takes on ideas, concepts, philosophical or moral categories, social or political phenomena, and so on.

Of course, the European novel has always, often with great generosity, lent itself to the expression of all kinds of ideas and reflections, but, particularly in works of the "second half," these are most often relegated to a secondary or subordinate position in relation to the narrative, which remains the center of the work, whereas these divagations are a kind of ornament or excrescence that may be more or less necessary. The most common and acceptable way to integrate them is to present them as utterances or thoughts issuing from some character, at some moment in his adventure—that is, as kinds of "intellectual events" tied to the unfolding of the story: it might be called the Dostoevskian technique. In fact, Kundera uses it in those of his novels where the novelist "I" almost never appears and where the essay-like passages then occur either as silent reflections or as part of dialogues, but attributed in either instance to some fictional character. This is so, for instance, in *Laughable Loves*, with Dr. Havel's "long speech" about the vanishing Don Juans, or, in *Farewell Waltz*, with the convivial conversation during which Bertlef and his guests expound their ideas about parenthood. Given that one of these guests—Jakub—is an intellectual, and thus particularly inclined toward reflection, many "essays" within the novel—on beauty, on innocence and guilt, on disgust and love in mankind—come through his thoughts, which often causes him, quite wrongly, to be considered the leading character of the novel, though he does not enter until the "Third Day."

In that same way—that is, within Jaroslav's monologue in Part Four of *The Joke*—the small musicological "treatise" on Moravian folk song occurs. But the "functional" nature of these pages is much less obvious, insofar as they comprise neither a commentary on the current action nor an expression of a character's frame of mind. In fact, their dramatic role is almost nil, and though the reader who skips them forgoes some essential information, he does not lose the thread of Jaroslav's story. In other words this chapter interrupts the narrative continuity by introducing an essay in the form of a digression, whose content concerns neither the novel's action and its progress, nor even the character's psychology, but some other dimension of the novel that would otherwise remain invisible—which not only justifies its presence but makes that presence absolutely necessary.

That said, the breach in the narrative framework remains somewhat veiled in this case by the fact that the essay is presented as an imaginary "speech" Jaroslav addresses to his absent son. It is much more evident in the works in which the novelist moves away from his characters and carves out his own space, makes his own voice heard alongside theirs in the novel's polyphonic "canon." This occurs as early as in the middle parts of *Life Is Elsewhere*, in which the story of Jaromil's tribulations is regularly interrupted, or rather accompanied, by "general" comments on poetry, youth, revolution. It also occurs, and even more strongly, in the last three Czech novels. Consider the author's reflections in *The Book of Laughter and Forgetting*, not only on the two words that give the novel its title but also on many other themes that stem from it: the acceleration of the historical process, graphomania, an image from an early story by Thomas Mann, "*litost*." Or consider the two opening chapters of *The Unbearable Lightness of Being*, in which, before any characters have entered the scene, there is a discussion of Nietzsche and Parmenides, the myth of eternal return, and the contradiction between the attributes of lightness and weight; or, in Part Six of that novel, the long exploration of the link between kitsch and shit. Or consider the remarks on the notion of imagology and on the figure *Homo sentimentalis* in Parts Three and Four of *Immortality*. Though not as extensive, essayistic digressions are just as frequent in *Slowness* (on hedonism, on "dancers," on glory and the feeling of "being among the elect," on a poem by Apollinaire) and again in *Ignorance* (on nostalgia, on Schoenberg, on the *Odyssey*). Everywhere, in short, the novelistic fabric is invaded, redoubled, constantly pierced by the meditations of the novelist, who appears as "philosopher," "musicologist," "lexicographer," "literary critic or theoretician," "anthropologist," or even "sociologist" nearly as often as he does as mere narrator.

The quotation marks immediately above are highly important. Because philosophy, musicology, or sociology are precisely what the "novelist's self" doesn't do. While the essays that enter the fabric of the novel may speak to what these disciplines consider to be their subjects, and

while they sometimes borrow elements of those vocabu-
laries, the method and aim here are obviously completely
different, if not contrary. The thinking that is being
worked out here, and the knowledge that results from it,
do not strive toward any general thesis, respect none of
the rules of reasoning or of "scientific" demonstration,
and are never subjected to the necessity of proving and
drawing a conclusion. Here the mode is one of undefined
open-mindedness and interrogation, of roaming and paradox—that is, of a perpetual quest down unpredictable
avenues, of some truth on the run that eludes any cap-
ture as it does any definitive formulation: like the words
Sabina and Franz exchange, it is a truth that can only be
"misunderstood"—that is, changeable, plural, uncertain.
In short, a *novelistic* truth.

And that is the way to read all the essays—or fragments of essays—that stud Kundera's novels, whether
they are thoughts or speeches attributed to characters, or
meditative passages in which the author himself speaks.
That the latter sometimes take on the neutral tone of
explanation and sometimes the more confidential one of
the "I" novelist's reflection or a recollection, or the tone
of social or political criticism, does not mean that they
differ fundamentally from the characters' ideas or that
they are any less part of the *fictional* and nonserious territory of the novel. For instance, even though it comes

directly from the novelist, without being mediated by a character, still the differential theory of the epic womanizer and the lyrical womanizer as expounded in a chapter of *The Unbearable Lightness of Being* is no more "objective" or more "valid" or of a different nature than Dr. Havel's theory of the Great Collector. In both cases we are reading what the author of *The Art of the Novel* calls a "specifically novelistic essay"—that is, a meditation "unthinkable outside the novel" that contains it and determines both its form and its content.

Not that these essays are lacking in cognitive scope or that the idea taking form in them fails to contribute to revealing and interpreting the world. Quite the contrary, the theory of the two varieties of womanizer or the theory of the Great Collector represents conceptual discoveries of incontestable value and beauty, just like the many other similar theories and definitions Kundera's novels put forward pertaining to categories aesthetic, erotic, moral, sociopolitical, and so on. Often paradoxical, imbued with great poetic and ironic force (both perhaps the same thing), these concepts and speculations, nevertheless, can in no case be isolated from their context and considered in the abstract, like intellectual entities valid in all times and places, without losing the essence of what defines them—that is, their rootedness in the concreteness of a particular existence—the character's—and of a world that is just as particular— the novel's. Existence and world whose complexity calls for the elucidating effort of the essay, but that in the last analysis always escapes, thus dooming novelistic thinking and any theory it can produce to insurmountable relativity and incompletion.

If it's true, as Kundera writes with a nod to Hermann Broch, that "a novel that does not discover a hitherto unknown segment of existence is immoral" and that "knowledge is the novel's only morality," it does not mean—far from it—that this knowledge is the same kind of thing as philosophical or scientific knowledge and must translate into verifiable and definitive propositions. This can only be a puzzled knowledge, riddled with things unknown, with contradictions, with fog; knowledge of the very unknowability of the world and of existence. But neither does it mean that the essays in a novel have any privileged standing or that they fulfill the epistemological mission of the novel better than any other element. What is distinctive about the "specifically novelistic" essay, on the contrary, even when it is presented as direct remarks by the novelist, is that it does not exist on its own, following solely its own logic, but that it always stands "within the magnetic field of a character," sometimes speaking what the character thinks or might think, and sometimes, Kundera writes in *The Art of the Novel*, "what happens inside my own head" when, observing the character, "I try, step by step, to get to the heart of his attitude, in order to understand it, name it, grasp it." Thus the essay is constantly interwoven in the stories with which it coexists within the novel. Interwoven, that is, supported, recommenced, nourished by them, but at the same time compromised and contradicted by their proximity and by its relations to them.

With most modern writers, when—it happens rather rarely—the author speaks in his own right and the narration gives way to an autonomous statement of certain ideas, that statement generally takes the form of a discourse more or less well incorporated into the rest of the work. Such, for example, are the reflections on the historiography rejected in the second part of the epilogue of *War and Peace*. Such, too, though the effort at integration there is more pronounced, is the treatise on the disintegration of values in the third part of Broch's *The Sleepwalkers*. As lucid as they are, on the architectonic and stylistic plane these speculative passages still largely remain foreign bodies within their respective novels, as if storytelling and thinking were two distinct and almost irreconcilable processes. In Kundera essays never occur all in one piece (as in Tolstoy) or as a series of specialized chapters (as in Broch), but rather as a scattered sequence of digressions and reflective pauses narrowly intertwined with the narrative sequence, itself intermittent and varied, which leads to two main consequences.

The first is that, by being merged in this way with the stories, the ideational framework is somewhat contaminated by them and itself takes on the quality of a story unfolding beside or inside the other ones. Relieved of the constraints and the rhetorical signs of argumentative discussion, it becomes a kind of intellectual tale whose protagonists are words, themes, notions just as unpredictable, as lively, as multifarious, prey to just as many transformations, exchanges, rejections, and conflicts—in short, just as "novelistic" as the novel's heroes. In *The Book of Laughter and Forgetting*, for instance, one of the most ubiquitous and enigmatic "characters," the one who turns up in every single one of the stories in diverse poses and under assorted faces—isn't it in fact this term, this idea: forgetting (and thus memory)? What exactly is "forgetting"—is it a misfortune or a benediction, should it be fought or embraced? No one can say upon closing the novel, any more than we can say, at the end of Tamina's story, if she is right to recall and then to forget her vanished husband.

The second consequence of interweaving novelistic essay with story is the close interdependence of the two forms, neither subordinate to the other. Sometimes it does happen that meditation seems to follow from narration, and to attach to it as "remarks" that clarify and complete it; sometimes, on the contrary, it happens that it is the narration that seems to obey the meditation and appears as an expansion of it. The leading role does not belong intrinsically to either one. Meditation and narration, essay and story, idea and life, go hand in hand here, and the driving force of the novel, like the knowledge it brings, is not entirely lodged either on one side or the other, neither in the characters' tribulations nor in the novelist's thoughts, but everywhere at once throughout the meditative narration (or narrative meditation) in which all parts of the work participate, each utterly whole and equal, like the several voices in a polyphonic song.

Thematic Unity

"There is room in a novel," Virginia Woolf writes, "for story-telling, for comedy, for tragedy, for criticism and information and philosophy and poetry. Something of its appeal lies in the width of its scope."* It could actually be said that it has always been a natural inclination of the novel—and the main reason for its vitality—to reject all "purity," all imprisonment in a canonical def-

---

*Virginia Woolf, *Granite and Rainbow* (London, 1929; reprint, 1958), p. 141.

inition of it and of its territory, and, on the contrary, never to cease colonizing the genres, the discourses, and the forms around it, however alien or refractory they appear to be, so as to incorporate them, turn them into its own substance, and, in doing so, to increase still more "the width of its scope." By freely multiplying the "lines" it gathers—unhindered by the diversity, indeed the heterogeneity that initially makes them seem incompatible with one another—Kunderian polyphony in a sense merely continues this age-old expansion, pushing it into regions hitherto considered impregnable. Nothing—no subject, no tone, no language—is a priori excluded from the novelistic universe—that is, stripped of polyphonic potentiality: neither the work of thought; neither historical, literary, nor musicological analysis; neither the personal experience of the novelist any more than the "unreality" of dreams or the "dialogues of the dead" to be heard in the fanciful realm of the immortals.

But this extension is not only, and not mainly, a matter of quantity. It has nothing to do with the simple gathering, in the novel's space, of unusual materials ever more numerous and heterogeneous, accumulated under the pretext of "hybridization" or "subversion," with the sole end of "deconstructing" discursive homogeneity and provoking the "explosion" of traditional codes, that is, "liberating" the novel from its own form. A principle of variety, of freedom and open-mindedness, Kunderian polyphony is anything but giving in to disorder. On the contrary, one might say that its fundamental contribution to the art of the novel is in fact to make at once possible and necessary to it the institution of such order—the most profound and rigorous order, while also the subtlest and lightest—which Kundera calls "thematic unity" and of which he makes a primary law of all his writing.

What does this law stipulate? How does it define thematic unity? At the first level (semantic, let's say), it simply designates the existence of a link of continuity between all the themes evoked by the novel, which is simply the place where they meet and exchange meanings. But in a broader sense, it also designates the presence in the oeuvre—in all parts of the oeuvre without exception, whatever their location, their dimensions, their genre, their narrative function, or their ontological or fictional status—of a common theme of which they are so many particular variations and that thereby makes them communicate among themselves and complement one another. What does this common theme consist of, what is the theme of this or that novel? To this question there is scarcely an answer possible other than a circular one: the theme of a novel is nothing more and nothing less than that novel itself—that is, the totality of the "lines" that comprise it and apart from which that theme cannot be defined or perhaps even exist—just as the mountain, for Agnès, is the location of her walk but cannot be perceived except by means of the paths running all over it. In other words the theme is not an external or prior premise, it cannot be isolated from its particular manifestations or formulated in terms other than those of the novel itself. *The Joke, Laughable Loves, The Book of Laughter and Forgetting, The Unbearable Lightness of Being, Immortality, Slowness, Identity, Ignorance*: all these titles of novels—as well as those of their parts: "The Angels," "The Border," "Soul and Body," "The Grand March," "The Face," "Fighting," "Chance," and so on—surely provide information, but they do not include any precise content, any statement that, once interpreted, would summarize—and thus replace—the text they designate. Their role is rather to delimit a terrain, to trace a semantic boundary within which the novel (or the part) develops by seeking a meaning that never ceases to move, to flee, to draw closer, to flee again, and to show itself regularly even as it slips off into endless metamorphoses. In short the theme of a novel is the blank center, indeterminable and yet ever present, to whose pull gravitate all the variations that constitute it, endlessly repeating and modifying themselves.

Consequently, but on the formal level this time, the law of thematic unity means that the composition of a novel rests mainly, if not exclusively, on its theme; that the theme—and not action, character, or setting—is what organizes the novel, what governs its whole architecture and thereby confers the cohesion necessary to its beauty and power.

In the history of the novel there is surely no work worthy of the name that does not in some way obey this law, that cannot also be read as the development of a theme or a group of themes binding its different parts to one another, making them illuminate one another and together contribute to produce a meaning that arises from each and at the same time surpasses all of them. In other words, thematic unity can be seen as one of the basic principles of all novelistic composition. But it is rarely the only or even the dominant principle, its presence and structural role most of the time making themselves felt as secondary, intermittent, as if they had to remain veiled or were there as *something extra*, content to accompany or underline such other much more decisive and obvious factors as unity of action, of character, of voice, or of setting, whose power is far greater than the theme's and inevitably relegates it to the background. The Kunderian law of thematic unity completely reverses that order. Not only does it make the theme appear openly but it also frees it from its subsidiary position by giving it the primary role in the inspiration and the writing of the work and in making it the most visible, the most immediate, and the most "constraining" element of the novelistic structure. A novel is thus no longer *also* an exploration of a theme; it is first and foremost—and ultimately nothing else but—that very exploration.

What does such a reversal signify? Two things especially. First, that all the parts of a novel—each narrative, descriptive, discursive, or other "molecule" that enters into its composition, no matter what dramatic or ideological necessity it fulfills besides, draws its existence, its meaning, and its value only from its relations with the thematic universe the novel seeks to elucidate. Thus it is both an exclusionary rule (anything that has no thematic function must be eliminated) and an opening to a vast space of new possibilities, since anything that can contribute to the enrichment or the clarification of the theme, anything that can make for a new variation, has its place in the novel.

Thematic unity, in short, is what frames and makes polyphonic proliferation possible; it organizes it and offers it room to open out; without it polyphony would only be cacophony. In return the multiplicity of genres, of voices, and of worlds is the best means for thematic unity; by its diversity, by the continual changes it introduces into the novel's texture, it not only feeds and enriches thematic development but also prevents attention from being interrupted, hypnotized by some one element, and thereby keeps the spotlight trained constantly on the presence and appeal of the theme that binds all the elements into one.

Giving priority to the requirements of thematic unity also leads—the second consequence—to an entirely new way of composing a novel. If it is defined primarily as a meditation on a theme, and if its unity mainly comes from that, then its form and its style can no longer follow the customary rules of the novel genre. The principal one of these usual rules, of course, is the rule of epic or dramatic unity, which has been—and widely remains—the great if not the only rule of the modern novel. The modern novel is thereby pressed to conceive of itself almost exclusively as a *narrative* art, focused on establishing and then unfolding a plot that is both unified (by the presence of a protagonist who is its subject) and continuous (by its taking place within time), and that progresses logically, through crises and tribulations, retreats and advances, toward the intended conclusion. Within this framework, many plots, many figures, often very complex and very beautiful, have been and continue to be invented; but the basic rule, however distorted or unrecognizable it may appear, is still nearly the same: without a story, without an orderly series of events—that is, without the tale of somebody's adventure or fate, a novel is not a novel, whatever the interest and abundance of all it otherwise contains.

The epic dimension—the account of the life of one or several characters—is far from absent in Kundera's novels. In the early Czech novels in particular—that is, in *The Joke*, *Life Is Elsewhere*, and *Farewell Waltz*—and then again in *Identity*, plot development occupies an important place and brings into play highly virtuosic strategies, which is also the case in the *Laughable Loves* stories as well as in certain strictly narrative parts of the novels themselves. So there is no novel by Kundera, not even those of the second section of the Czech cycle, including *The Book of Laughter and Forgetting*, that can be said to lack characters and action, in the way the "*nouveau roman*" claimed to do. *The Unbearable Lightness of Being* is also the story of Tomas and Tereza, of Sabina and Franz; *Immortality* is also that of Agnès, of Laura, of Paul, of Rubens. The originality of Kunderian art consists not in destroying the epic principle but in stripping it of its sovereignty, and this principle that customarily subjects everything else to its law is itself subjected to the new law—thematic unity—and after having been master thereby becomes one of its servants.

This dethronement of plot is expressed in three ways:

First, in the overall composition of the novel, by the

refusal to give to the action—that is, to the account of the characters' gestures, words, or thoughts and to the narration of events that happen to them, as dramatic and captivating as this material might be—any precedence over the other elements of the work, which get the same treatment, the same care, the same essential position in its organization, in conformity with what polyphonic *equality* requires.

Second, and this time inside the story, by the disappearance—according to the same rule of equality—of a single or principal action that unfolds constantly from beginning to end, in favor of setting up, as I've already noted, a cluster of multiple, interconnected actions that are often independent or purely circumstantial with regard to one another, but none of which can be called central and the others secondary or auxiliary. This is equally true of the characters, among whom there is no real "hero"—that is, a single or principal protagonist whose destiny alone governs the entire plot of the novel and to whom the other characters only serve as "opponents" or "allies" more or less devoid of their own existence, consciousness, and worth.

And, third, by the abandonment or at least the devaluation, in the narrative itself, of the usual structure that is based on a logical-temporal series linking events and their ranking according to the role of each in the sequence of causes and effects, by which dramatic unity and progress build with the most verisimilitude. Instead, Kunderian narration readily welcomes "chance," "coincidence"—that is, rifts and interruptions in causality—as well as it retains detail and anecdote rather than the meticulously prepared "big scene." The narration is interested in actions or events not for their dramatic significance but for their thematic value; that is, for the semantic or figurative connection that ties them not only to other more or less distant actions or events—even more or less foreign to the particular narrative line of which they themselves are a part—but also to all the nonnarrative parts of the work.

The Rehabilitation of Episode

All novelistic action, in short, tends to be treated as an "episode," as a more or less fortuitous event, occurring, as a passage in *Immortality* says, "outside the causal chain of events that is the story," and thus able to "be left out without making the story lose its intelligible continuity." Now, a Kunderian story, far from avoiding them, purposely seeks such "unessential" events, and if it attaches to them, it is because their omission, which would help the action's continuity, would by contrast risk harming or eclipsing the most precious dimension of the work and rendering "unintelligible" the essence of its meaning. Indifferent or injurious to the development of the story that it unduly delays or suspends, episode, in other words, becomes absolutely necessary to the revelation of theme.

Among the most beautiful examples is of course Part Six of *Life Is Elsewhere*, whose content can no longer add to Jaromil's *story* because it unfolds after his death. But this interlude on the life of the man in his forties maintains an essential contrapuntal relation with the Jaromil *theme*, from which comes the requirement to tell the story before the one about the poet's death. Just as striking in this regard, if not more so, are Part Six of *Immortality*, which recounts the affair between Rubens and Agnès, and Part Seven of *The Unbearable Lightness of Being*, in which Tomas and Tereza, withdrawn to the country, look after their ailing dog. Unlike the one on the man in his forties, these sequences present characters whose existence occupies an important place in the rest of the novel. But their episodic nature is all the more apparent: they are both *posthumous*—they are narrated after the reader has already learned of the aforesaid characters' deaths (Agnès's is the subject of a detailed account in Part Five of the novel; Tomas and Tereza's are indicated in Part Three and again in Part Six). These events (the rendezvous with Rubens, Karenin's smiles) were therefore not at all necessary for understanding the characters' fates, within which the events play no particular role, neither as cause nor as effect of any other event, not even of their deaths; they are "pure" events that happen to the characters, entirely "outside the causal chain of events that is [their] story." If the novel nevertheless lingers over them, if it invites the reader— who is already cognizant of the plot sequence and of the fates of Agnès and that of Tomas and Tereza—to linger over them as well, despite their functionally secondary or superfluous nature, and if he does so exactly at the moment of its unfolding, it is because these episodes, these narrative "sidesteps" that divert the story from its straight way, at the same time sequester—and for that very reason—invaluable deposits of meaning. It is as if the novel, liberated from its obligations as epic (the logical and continuous development of the story), might then freely commit itself to its primary law, the call of its theme, and as if a well were suddenly opening to let its deepest possibilities flow to the surface.

No novel, however, better illustrates this rehabilitation of episode than *The Book of Laughter and Forgetting*, in which, as Kundera himself writes, "unity of action is entirely replaced by unity of themes,"* that is, in

---

*Chvatik, *Le Monde romanesque de Milan Kundera*, p. 243.

which the composition—"in the form of variations"—
rests entirely on the reprise and the deepening of one and
the same thematic complex, apart from any plot, any central and continuous action that links the various parts of
the novel. No causal or temporal relationship actually
exists between them, except, minimally, between Parts
Four and Six, which unfold in the same setting, present
the same character, Tamina, and can thus be read as two
successive moments of her story. For the rest, every particular story, every adventure—Mirek's in "Lost Letters,"
Karel's in "Mama," that of Gabrielle, Michelle, and
Sarah in "The Angels," of the student in "Litost," or of
Jan in "The Border"—from the dramatic point of view
constitute episodes in the pure state, all the more "gratu-
itous" in that there is no shared plot here to connect them
to; these feel, one might say, like parentheses in a sentence
that has been erased. But only in a *narrative* sentence.
Because these parentheses also form a different sentence—this one *thematic*—in which each parenthesis
plays an irreplaceable role; but the syntax that binds
them together is of another kind than the one novels customarily utilize.

Of this new syntax, *The Book of Laughter and For-*
getting is indisputably the boldest realization in Kundera's
oeuvre, making this novel a kind of borderline work. But
it is also, here again, a pivotal work, for this devaluation

of epic in favor of thematic requirements will again mark the two next novels, *The Unbearable Lightness of Being* and *Immortality*, in which it takes less extreme forms, perhaps, but will no less govern the whole of the composition, which will again be the case, on a more concentrated and "quicker" scale, in *Slowness* and in *Ignorance*. *The Book of Laughter and Forgetting* is also a pivotal work in that it casts a retrospective light on the preceding novels, in which the thematic syntax may not stand forth but is also at work there, and is just as powerful, if not more powerful, in determining the story's organization and course as is the logic of epic. In *Testaments Betrayed*, Kundera says that he undertook to write *The Book of Laughter and Forgetting* as "a kind of second volume of *Laughable Loves*," but soon saw that he "was writing an entirely different thing," a novel built precisely on thematic unity alone. But then this discovery has a retrospective effect, in turn, on his view of *Laughable Loves*, whose composition in the form of a collection he now sees as a "prefiguration" of the new aesthetic deployed in *The Book of Laughter and Forgetting*. This kind of rereading can also apply very nicely to *The Joke*, to *Life Is Elsewhere*, or to a work whose dramatic cohesion is as tight as that of *Farewell Waltz*. Even if the continuity of action in them is more obvious, even if the narration seems more consonant with chronological and causal order, these novels in their way are no less constructed "in the form of variations": not only are "episodes" frequent (for example, in *The Joke*, the love story of Ludvik and Lucie, or in Kostka's monologue), but every moment of the action, every scene, even those most necessary for the logical development of the story, also—*at the same time*—contributes to the "development," to the resumption and deepening of a theme, of a meditation, of a series of "existential questions that, illuminated from different angles, run through the entire novel."*

The Art of the Chapter

Using the term "syntax" to describe this new art of novelistic composition can give rise to confusion, insofar as this word mainly describes a type of linear articulation (notably that of successive elements in a sentence). It is precisely the particular feature of the "path-novel," based on polyphonic heterogeneity and thematic unity, to forgo any linearity, any horizontality, and to present itself less as a linked chain than as an *array*, as a multi-dimensional *space* inside which semantic and formal connections are made, literally, *in all directions*: from before to after, from part to whole, but also from after

*Chvatik, *Le Monde romanesque de Milan Kundera*, p. 243.

to before, from whole to part, and from each part to each other part. "In a great novel," Julien Gracq observes, "unlike the imperfectly consistent world of reality, nothing remains *marginal*—juxtaposition never occurs anywhere, connection occurs everywhere. . . . Like an organism, a novel lives by proliferating *exchanges*. . . . Its method is to create a homogeneous environment, a novelistic ether in which people and things are steeped and which send vibrations through all the senses."*

If the Kunderian novel is very much indebted to music in this way, as the novelist himself has often declared, its architectural principle is also very close to that art par excellence of "vibrations," "exchanges," and nonlinear relations that is poetry. Indeed, in a poetic text, meaning and beauty—indistinguishable one from the other—come less from the sequence of words, images, and sounds—from the vanishing of one to make room for the next ("juxtaposition"), than from their simultaneous presence in a kind of landscape constantly composed and recomposed by the harmonies, the contrasts, and the affinities that make each one a variation—meaning: a repetition and a transformation—of all the others, from the nearest to the most

---

*Julien Gracq, *Lettrines* (1967), in *Oeuvres complètes*, vol. 2 (Paris, "Bibliothèque de la Pléiade," 1995), pp. 149–50 (italics in original).

remote (the "connection"). This is just the type of reading—rather, of constant *rereading*—that the path-novel
calls for, reading in which it is not a matter of rushing
to the conclusion but of walking slowly in the middle
of a forest whose form is "continuous and constantly
changing," full of stops and detours and side paths and
a succession of views and echoes at once unexpected
and familiar. So however much the author of *Life Is
Elsewhere* is considered to be an enemy of poets, his art
as a novelist is an homage to the powers and the inven-
tions of poetry.

Like poetry, moreover, it is not only the aesthetic
of "spatial" composition but also the type of writing
that the Kunderian novel utilizes: writing that itself is
nonlinear, splintered, fond of ellipses, interruptions,
abrupt shifts, and that, rather than trying to manufac-
ture a text all of a single piece, so to speak, composes
it as a mosaic of discrete and varied elements, well
separated from one another, at once complete in themselves and unified by multiple connections and contrasts that the reader must incessantly discover, as we
do in fact when we read a poem or an only slightly
structured collection of poems. Closer to *Tristram
Shandy* and to picaresque novels than to the modern
way (Balzacian, Proustian, or Joycean, for instance) of
composing a novel in long, equal, and continuous

"flows,"* this discontinuity technique is certainly, on the formal level, another of the most consistent and striking features of Kundera's novels. It fulfills the double requirement of multiplicity and unity at the same time. The fact of working the novel's matter by fragments, of increasing the number of breaks and pauses, is a means not only to make clearer distinctions among the various "lines" that comprise it but above all to treat them with as thorough an equality and simultaneity as possible, while keeping all of them constantly "active," able to intersect or replace one another at any time. The technique of discontinuous writing, in short, is the very means of polyphonic continuity.

In the seven Czech novels, it appears first in the division into parts. As we know, these always come in odd numbers (seven or five) and (except in *Farewell Waltz*) each part is announced by a title that identifies its main theme. Within any one novel they may be relatively equal in length (as in *The Book of Laughter and Forgetting*) or, more often, variable, which allows diverse effects of relief and equilibrium. But unlike what occurs in most novels arranged in parts, the division here follows not only or mainly considerations of chronology or

---

*For statistics fans let's note that the 495 pages of Sterne's novel (in the Harvard edition) are divided into nine "volumes" and 312 "chapters"; that *Gil Blas* consists of twelve "books" and 133 chapters; and that there are eighteen books and 208 chapters in *Tom Jones*.

material (one or several primary characters, or the era, or recounted events, and so on) but also—and perhaps even more—certain formal considerations, each part standing apart from its neighbors by differences of length, dominant style (narrative or essayistic), manner (sarcastic, neutral, or emotional), rhythm, and the like. So much so that to go from one part to the other is to enter a new, often unpredictable terrain, where the temporality, the ambience, the topography have suddenly changed, but where nevertheless the same "novelistic ether" circulates, constantly enriched, inexhaustible.

Cutting up a novel into parts is, however, only an initial aspect—the most external, one might say, of that discontinuity. More noteworthy still is the existence of a second level of articulation involving an additional fragmenting of the text: the division of each part into small sequences that Kundera calls "chapters." Well separated from one another, and identified by numbers or titles, these sequences constitute the basic unit of Kunderian writing, which explains why we also find them (numbered into the fifties each time) in the three French novels, which are too short to be divided into "parts,"* and right up to *The Art of the Novel* and *Testaments Betrayed*, books that are themselves based, espe-

---

*Conspicuous in this regard are Part One of *The Joke*, which is not divided into chapters, and "Symposium," which, though it forms the fourth part of *Laughable Loves*, is divided into five "acts," themselves divided into thirty-seven titled sequences (or scenes).

cially the latter, on the polyphonic deployment of thought, and that might therefore be called "path-essays."

By the combinations to which it lends itself, the division of every part into chapters allows the construction of highly diversified architectures. Let's take a single example, that of *The Unbearable Lightness of Being*. Its three even-numbered parts (Two, Four, and Six) contain not only the greatest number but also exactly the same number of chapters (twenty-nine), while the odd-numbered parts respectively include seventeen (Part One), eleven (Part Three), twenty-three (Part Five), and as few as seven (Part Seven). Besides, even if the length of the chapters varies considerably within the novel (the longest run somewhat less than ten pages, the shortest less than one), that is not the case within each part, where, whatever their number, they deviate little from a common average length: nearly two pages in Part One, a bit more than four in Part Three, around five in the seven chapters of Part Seven. Combining one with the other, these different "variables" (length of part, number of chapters, average length of chapters) imbue each part with a very particular emotional climate and rhythm: two parts of the same length, depending on whether they are divided into many short chapters or into a small number of longer ones, will not produce the same effect or color their meaning in the same way. Thus, still in *The Unbearable Lightness of*

Being, the first and last parts may indeed have the same number of pages (thirty-two), but the one divided into seventeen chapters and the other into seven create between them a relationship of opposition—of fast to slow, of light to serious—that reinforce and bring out even more clearly what the novel elsewhere tells us about Tomas's development. Conversely, the structural kinship tying Parts Two and Four, each of which runs forty pages divided into twenty-nine chapters, compels us to "see" what the novel this time does not "say"—that is, the hidden parallel linking Tereza's existence to that of Franz, about whom she knows nothing.*

Considered in isolation, the Kunderian chapter is characterized by its extreme condensation, its tendency toward brevity, and its maximal expressivity. That is primarily how it can be compared to a poem: in a few pages, indeed in a few sentences, it comes as a complete small universe, whose content might be a scene, an idea, an image, indeed just a single gesture, a word, an isolated remark. It is sometimes dynamic, sometimes static, here making action leap ahead or meditation advance toward a new stage, there interrupting it better to deepen it; but always it is carefully circumscribed and saturated with meaning.

With meaning and with formal necessity. Because

---

*On the effects of the division into parts and chapters, notably in *Life Is Elsewhere*, see *The Art of the Novel*, Part Four, pp. 87–89.

each chapter, without exception, is conceived so as to play an absolutely indispensable role in the structure of the novel and the development of its theme. They are so brief and numerous because all the fasteners and scaffoldings between them have vanished—everything that in the conventional novel does not directly contribute to the meaning but arises solely from the mechanics of linking: skillfully managed transitions, preparations, foreshadowings, justifications, and all those more or less artificial maneuvers aimed at furthering the plausibility or the apparent logic of the text. But on the contrary, here all sorts of discontinuities are permitted from chapter to chapter: utterly unexpected ellipses and digressions, abrupt breaks, deep rifts—the only concern being that the thematic tension never sag. Like many excellent novelists, Mario Vargas Llosa considers it inevitable that a novel have a fairly large proportion of "dead time, of episodes . . . with nothing more than a linking function," in other words, of filler: "Poetry," he writes in *Letters to a Young Novelist*, "may be an intensive genre, distilled to the essentials, without waste. The novel may not." In Kunderian art the purpose of the small chapter is precisely to rid the novel of such waste—Breton called it those "empty moments"—so that it may, like poetry, never "stray by even a single line from what he cares about, what fascinates him"

(*Testaments Betrayed*) while "holding on to only the essential."*

On the level of style this requirement presumes the use of compact language as spare and direct as possible—qualities that are entirely opposite to those we ordinarily associate with "poetic prose," made up most often, as Alain wrote about what he called "the ornate style," "of appearances, almost like apparitions or visions, each word sparkling and dancing for its own sake, or else forming into games and ring dances with its neighbors." Kundera's prose is a rigorously "prosaic" one. It avoids like the plague approximations and surface effects, surprises, coyness, lexical or grammatical transgressions—that whole modern cult of "writing" and of the "work of the signifier" that claims to emancipate language by assigning it no aim but its own shimmer. Here, on the contrary, the style has a classic tinge to it; entirely dedicated to the meaning it must transmit, it is an essentially modest style that tends toward the bareness and clarity of aphorism. "My language seeks to be simple, precise, as if transparent, and to be such in every translation,"† the novelist declares. To that end every paragraph, every sentence, every word, every punctua-

---

*Kundera, "Savoir rester dans l'essentiel—à propos de *Retours et autres pertes* de Sylvie Richterova," *L'Atelier du roman* (November 1993), p. 91.
†Kundera, "La frontière invisible," written dialogue with Guy Scarpetta, *Le Nouvel Observateur,* January 15–21, 1998.

tion mark is not only chosen with care, calculated, strictly motivated; it is also exemplary in its clarity and economy. Which is what makes the author of *Immortality* say, with less exaggeration than it seems: "If a reader skips a single sentence of my novel he won't be able to understand it."

Instead of such cursory, rapid reading, to which novels generally lend themselves, the segmentation of the text and the precision of the writing thus ask of Kundera's reader an attention—that is, an examination and an effort at interpretation—that stands alert to the slightest sign, the slightest shift, the slightest detail, for fear that "the essential" might escape him. For such reading, tinged both with *slowness* (by the frequent pauses created by the division into parts and chapters) and with an unceasing density (by the weighty significance of every fragment and every word), one of the closest models would probably be the several hours spent together by Vivant Denon's lovers: hours that, "by slowing the course of their night, by dividing it into different stages, each separate from the next," and by imprinting on each the purest form, Madame de T. fashions into a little masterpiece of seduction and bliss. But again, the model could also well be Agnès's last walk on the mountain paths that afternoon.

Repose

As God slowly departed from the seat whence he had directed the universe and its order of values, distinguished good from evil, and endowed each thing with meaning, Don Quixote set forth from his house into a world he could no longer recognize.

MILAN KUNDERA

What happens to Agnès during her walk? Does she follow a particular route? Is she looking for undergrowth or open views? Is she discovering flowers, trees, animals she never knew before? Does she see, from the Goethe poem that lulled her in childhood, the "birds in the woods . . . silent"? The novel doesn't say. All we know is that Agnès spends the final afternoon of her life entirely in the tranquillity and withdrawal that is given her by the simple fact of being alone on "paths secluded from the world," with no witness, no family, and as if no homeland. For the rest, it is a perfectly neutral episode in which nothing takes place other than the passage of several unchanging and lost hours. Or rather, yes, a small event does take place, but it is all the less an event, properly speaking, for being unaccompanied by any action or followed by any consequence other than a "special moment" during which everything is immobilized and seems to be suspended:

> She reached the bank of a stream and lay down in the grass. She lay there for a long time and had the feeling that the stream was flowing into her, washing away all her hurt and dirt: washing away her self. A special, unforgettable moment: she was forgetting her self, losing her self, she was without a self; and that was happiness.

At the time Agnès is not really aware of what has happened to her. It is only several hours later, at the wheel of her car, barely a few minutes before the accident that will kill her, that the moment experienced that afternoon comes back to mind and she takes the time to reflect on it:

> In recalling this moment, an idea came to Agnès, vague and fleeting and yet so very important, perhaps supremely important, that she tried to capture it for herself in words:
>
> What is unbearable in life is not *being* but *being one's self*. The Creator, with his computer, released

into the world billions of selves as well as their lives. But apart from this quantity of lives it is possible to imagine some primordial being that was present even before the Creator began to create, a being that was—and still is—beyond his influence. When she lay on the ground that day and the monotonous song of the stream flowed into her, cleansing her of the self, the dirt of the self, she participated in that primordial being, which manifested itself in the voice of fleeting time and the blue of the sky; she now knows there is nothing more beautiful.

Here I reach the third and last stage of the critical investigation that has had me shadowing Agnès's footsteps from the start. This third stage, it's true, does not follow the first two, since it takes place *during* Agnès's walk, of which it represents neither the conclusion nor the continuation but merely a "moment." A privileged moment, however, because concentrated there like an emblem is the deep meaning not only of her walk but also of her entire existence, which has been nothing other than waiting, than the slow genesis of that instant of lucidity and peace.

From the beginning of the novel, in fact, one of the first things we learn about Agnès is that she lives in mourning for her father, who died five years earlier, and that this mourning is tied to the Swiss landscape where, she says, "there were paths in those forests; her father stood on one of them, smiling and inviting her to join him." Her father was to her a man of silence and suppression, the destroyer of photographs, the enemy of gazing and of fighting, the antihero seeking only to flee, to withdraw, to "leave slowly, unseen, for a world without faces." So the "special moment" experienced on the edge of the stream marks reunion with her father, that is, the fulfillment of the desire that has haunted Agnès's entire novelistic life: the desire to escape a body, a face, gestures, a name that oblige her to carry the burden of an identity she doesn't want and that crucifies her, that tyrannizes her and that, despite her wishes, hands her over to the gaze and the pursuits of other people. Not that she suffers from being the woman she is or that she would wish to be different or better. Her desire, her "fatigue," is far deeper than that. It is not a matter of changing the self but rather of seeing her self obliterated, all the features of her self, those she has taken on as well as those she has been given, a matter of "subtracting" them from herself one after the other until she has no self left—until she is not only without a mask but also without a face, without a name, absent, vanished. Such, that afternoon, is the grace she is momentarily granted: subtraction finally ending in zero, the mirror blank, Agnès ceasing to be Agnès.

This scene, with its mystical tones, which recalls the emergence of the Platonic philosopher from the cave of appearances, could be compared to a moment of illumination or of "ecstasy"* if its content were not essentially *negative*. For Agnès's experience is not so much one of stretching of the self to the size of the landscape as one of forgetting, the nullification of all subjectivity. The difference is important. Certainly, the repose and the "happiness" this experience brings Agnès come from the calming—at least momentarily—of the conflict between soul and world. But here the calming does not follow from a victory of the self over the hostility or strangeness of the world—as occurs, for example, in the reveries of Rousseau's solitary walker, who feels "consolation, hope, and peace" because nature finally allows him to be "occupied only with [his] self." Such is also the quality of reverie according to Gaston Bachelard: it plunges the subject into "a world homogeneous with his being, . . . an *inside* which has no *outside*," where "the world no longer poses any opposition to him," where "the I no longer opposes itself to the world," but where, on the contrary, "there is no more non-self." These interludes of fusion between self and world Georg Lukács calls "lyrical moments" to indicate their exceptional nature in the novel's context; then, he writes, "the purest interiority of

*About this word, see *Testaments Betrayed*, pp. 82–84.

the soul, . . . lifted above the obscurely determined multiplicity of things, solidifies into substance; whilst alien,
unknowable nature is driven from within, to agglomerate
into a symbol that is illuminated throughout," so that the
external world "is only a sensually perceptible projection
of the essential—of interiority." Now, Agnès's peace on
the bank of the stream is made of something entirely different: if the conflict between the world and the self seems
to break off, it is not because the latter miraculously rec-
ognizes itself in the former and "there is no longer a non-
self"; on the contrary it is because all subjectivity is abolished, dissolved, "washed away" by the stream and there
is no longer anything—nothing—but the non-self.

The Novelistic Moment

Agnès's repose therefore arises from a separation, an exile.
It is the repose of someone who is drawing away from herself and from the world, of someone turning her back and
vanishing. This retreat, this emigration I will call—to distinguish it clearly from a "lyrical moment"—a novelistic
moment. It represents the impulse that opens the mental
and ontological space which is the distinctive locale of the
Kunderian novel or, rather its "non-place," for it is a space
that is defined only by the *distance* that constitutes it.
Indeed, in Kundera the novel is always written from the

edges of the world. It is always a work of desertion, at once the search for and the achievement of a radical, definitive rupture by which the world and its beings appear in a light that feels like dusk, alien, problematic, as if unburdened of their substance and, now comic, now pitiable, on the point of vanishing into nonsense at any moment. It is as if the gaze that grips them was already the gaze of a person who no longer belongs to them.

That is why what happens to Agnès is not an isolated case—far from it. Each of Kundera's novels takes pains to reproduce, from various angles and fictitious contexts, the founding experience that the novelistic moment is, as if the goal were to deepen the meaning by incessant variations and to constantly reenact before the mind's eye the first wrenching off, the ontological ripping away that makes it what it is.

Two sets of examples can be given here according to the aspect under which the occurrence is represented: either in the course of its occurring or as already occurred. It is primarily in the novels of the Czech cycle that we find the first group of cases, which have in common that the novelistic moment is shown there as a kind of awakening in which the character, until then caught up in his story, frees himself from it and from himself so as to see them from the outside and suddenly discover their vanity. And so this disillusionment often takes place toward the end of the story, as a kind of ironic anti-conclusion that undercuts the meaning and the value of everything the character has experienced and all that has happened to him. It is what occurs when the narrator of "Nobody Will Laugh," in the opening part of *Laughable Loves*, realizes that his stratagems and his lies have only made him a plaything of events he had thought he ruled:

> All at once I understood that it had only been my illusion that we ourselves saddle events and control their course; the truth is that they aren't *our* stories at all, that they are foisted on us from somewhere *outside*; that in no way do they represent us; that we are not to blame for the strange paths they follow; that they are themselves directed from who knows where by who knows what strange forces.

It's true that Klara's lover is a loser and that his story fails from start to finish: his girlfriend leaves him and he loses his job. But that isn't the case with Eduard, the character in the last part of the book, for whom, on the contrary, everything seems to succeed, seeing that he gains his political security and ends up in bed with Alice. And yet he too is faced by a similar revelation when at the end he "sadly" realizes that "the love adventure he had experienced . . . was derisory, made up of chance and errors, without any seriousness or meaning," that Alice's words and gestures were only "signs devoid of significance, currency without backing, weights made of paper," and that he himself had only been "a shadow of all these shadow-characters" among whom his story unfolded.

"Awakening," "revelation": these words only very imperfectly say what is at issue, which has nothing to do with the disclosure of some hitherto hidden secret. In fact, what Eduard and, in his way, Klara's lover, discover is not a truth, still less *the* truth, but rather the nonexistence of any truth, and therefore their own blindness. Awareness here is not a gain but a loss; far from putting an end to illusion, it confirms the very impossibility of putting an end there.

Their discovery, in short, is the contrary of an elevation toward the light. It is a darkening, a fall, the sudden collapse of all reference points as of all values. No character experiences that descent more intensely than Ludvik, toward the end of *The Joke*, when he understands to what degree "the *entire* story of [his] life was conceived in error." Not only had he been sentenced in error, not only had he loved and then abandoned Lucie in error but also even his revenge itself—that is, his efforts to correct the initial error and settle his scores with the past—only precipitated him into a new error, so that all the meaning he wanted to give to his life and all the power he thought he had over his actions collapsed like a house of cards. Here is the joker, the lover of "beautiful demolitions," the rectifier of History's wrongs, discovering himself as both victim and instrument of a scheme all the more insane for being without an originator, without a reason, and therefore without appeal. "And then I realized how powerless I was to revoke my own joke when throughout my life as a whole I was involved in a joke much more vast (all-embracing for me) and utterly irrevocable."

"What if History plays jokes?" Ludvik wonders. And what if the world itself were playing jokes, what if it had become no more than a trap, an immense sham? And what if love were just a long series of misunderstandings? And if there were no justice, "no difference between the guilty and the victims," and "the persecuted [were] no better than the persecutors," as Jakub discovers in *Farewell Waltz*? And if all values were merely optical illusion? And if there were no truth, that all signs were adrift and could take no matter what meanings? And what if, as Tereza thinks, "all things and people seemed to go about in disguise," and under this disguise there were only a second disguise, then still another, and so on to infinity, and it were then impossible ever to encounter anything other than masks, impersonations, cardboard settings? And what if living in the midst of all this therefore inevitably meant deceiving, being mistaken, being deceived? The novelistic moment is the moment when these diabolical questions crop up and when by that very fact, everything is shaken and threatened with ruin. In other words, already devastated.

Jakub also asks this sort of question at the end of *Farewell Waltz*, when Kamila's stunning beauty, seen that morning, and Skreta's confidences about his project of "fraternal" insemination lead him to think about his long life as an activist, whose meaning suddenly weakens, breaks up, and topples into nothingness:

> He had the strange feeling of having lived in his own country without knowing what was happening in it. . . . He always believed he was hearing the heartbeat of the country. But who knows what he was really hearing? Was it a heart? Or was it an old alarm clock? An old discarded alarm clock that gives the wrong time? Had all his political struggles been anything more than will-o'-the wisps distracting him from what really mattered? . . .
>
> What if he had been living in a world entirely different from what he imagined? What if he had been seeing everything upside down?

With the meditations that occupy him throughout that "Fifth" and last "Day" of the novel, Jakub seems to be the most "oedipal" of Kundera's characters. Just as much as Eduard's, Ludvik's, or the narrator's of "Nobody Will Laugh," but still more insistently, his ultimate recog-

nition directly recalls Sophocles' hero coming to understand with horror that he has lived from the start as a
man "seeing nothing, knowing nothing" of the person he
was and the crimes he committed. But whereas Oedipus
gouges out his eyes because he finally sees the truth dazzling him and thereby frees himself from his own blindness, Jakub's questioning only dissolves, one after
another, the truths he considers himself to be attached to
and thrusts him into a still deeper darkness. The "tragic
moment," one might say, occurs when the hero hears the
answer that judges his actions and obliterates all questions; the novelistic moment, on the contrary, is when all
the answers slip away, when all judgment is suspended
and when the hero sees the infinite extent of doubt and
uncertainty.

Jakub's belated "conversion," just like Ludvik's, is
therefore not only—or mainly—about the political ideas
he had defended, which had "nearly cost him his life,"
however noble and sincere they may have been. It is politics itself, it is every form of political idea and political
battle, and it is—more radically still—any undertaking,
in a world that is suddenly devalued, emptied of its substance and therefore struck with an "irrevocable" *unbelief*, because once suspicion enters—that is, once the
chasm has begun to gape between the person and himself,
between the person and the world—there is no longer

any way to go back and regain lost faith and innocence. From the instant a runner has dropped out of the race he can no longer rejoin it; his defection is irreparable.

Whether its subject is history and politics (Jakub), personal life (Eduard, Klara's lover), or both at once (Ludvik), a character's "dissidence" always brings on the ruin of everything that had served as a basis for his identity and had given the sequence of his actions, his desires, and his thoughts the appearance of a "biography": an order, a logic, and a meaning. He is, literally, outside himself as he is outside the world; any contract that had bound him to this or that identity or made him a supporter of this or that value is broken, since he now sees that any identity, like any value, is inevitably unstable, arbitrary, susceptible at any moment to turning into its opposite, and therefore undeserving of the slightest trust, the slightest attachment. Although he knows, like Jakub, that "he had no other," the world has ceased to be his homeland.

Jakub will soon be stateless, and these reflections cross his mind at the very moment when he is preparing to leave his country, as if they were inspired by the proximity of the border. Jan, the character in the last part of *The Book of Laughter and Forgetting*, has already emigrated, but all of his thought and existence remain snagged, fascinated by "the word 'border,' [which] in its common geographical sense reminds him of another border, an intangible and immaterial border" in which can be seen, once again, an image of what I am trying somehow to define. The novelistic moment, I might say, drawing on Jan's meditations, is the moment when the "border" is perhaps not crossed but at least becomes visible—which perhaps may be basically the same thing. But Jan wonders what border we are talking about, recalling "the woman he had loved most" telling him "that she held on to life by a thread":

> Yes, she did want to live, life gave her great joy, but she also knew that her "I want to live" was spun from the threads of a spiderweb. It takes so little, so infinitely little, for someone to find himself on the other side of the border, where everything—love, convictions, faith, history—no longer has meaning. The whole mystery of human life resides in the fact that it is spent in the immediate proximity of, and even in direct contact with, that border, that it is separated from it not by kilometers but by barely a millimeter.

"It takes so little," he indicates later on, "a tiny puff of air, for things to shift imperceptibly, and whatever it was that a man was ready to lay down his life for a few seconds earlier seems suddenly to be sheer nonsense." Jan constantly comes up against that concept of the border—that threat, that imminence of the breakdown of meaning. It is neither in politics (like Jakub) nor in history (like Ludvik) that Jan in fact comes to experience it, but initially on the most intimate terrain, that of love, which little by little becomes for this womanizer a terrain disenchanted by repetition. One day when he tries to make a conquest of a young, beautiful stranger glimpsed on a train, he realizes that his strategies merely imitate one another from one woman to another and that "all imitation was worthless." "He saw the pitiful pantomime of his gaze and gesture, that stereotyped gesticulation emptied of all meaning by years of repetition." Thus repetition, making things each time "lose a fraction of their meaning," ends up emptying them. The border then becomes so clear, so near, that one can no longer, as it were, hold back from crossing it.

The Libertine

If the duty of "apprehending the real world is part of the definition of the novel," as the author of *Testaments Betrayed* reminds us, the Kunderian novel, I might say, is the world and existence apprehended "from the other side of the border, where things no longer have meaning" and from where, as a consequence, all things can only appear as ambiguity and chaos, a mug's game and madhouse of fakery.

The characters just mentioned have led us to the immediate vicinity of the border. Each in his way has discovered its presence—and considered the effects of this discovery—but not yet crossed it. It is another group of characters whom we will now ask: What happens once you cross the border? How do you live when the world is no longer your homeland?

To this question—the modern question par excellence—two answers are possible, corresponding to the two great Kunderian novelistic modes of irony and imagination, as they are illustrated—or better, questioned—by some of the oeuvre's strongest figures. The first—and most often commented on—is the one I would call the satanic mode. It consists, once the border is crossed (or seen), of returning to the world and staying there, but having ceased to belong to it and considering it not so much a hell for suffering as a farce for laughter.

"Only after a while," says Klara's lover at the very end of his affair, "did it occur to me (in spite of the chilly silence that surrounded me) that my story was not of the tragic sort, but rather of the comic variety." Tragedy, in fact, just like rebellion (or revolution) is grounded on a serious vision of the world and of life; that is, on the belief in an order (metaphysical or moral) whose absence, or at least diminution, is felt as an attack against justice and thus requires some reparation, which, if it comes, will restore the disrupted order and, if not, will bring on destruction and despair. That is not at all the perspective that their border awareness inspires in Kundera's "satanic characters," who are to tragic heroes what the fatalist Jacques is to Oedipus or Havel to Don Juan: individuals ending up "in a domain . . . where everything is possible and everything is permitted." For them the world's disorder is its very essence and no mere accident, illusion, or temporary imbalance to which they are consenting or rebellious victims. Truth, justice, meaning are not only obscured, they are forever lost. All that survives are remnants of truth, parodies of justice, and semblances of meaning that we need not deplore or inveigh against (in the name of what?) but quite simply recognize and inhabit for what they are: the laughable remains of a world at an end, itself all the more laughable in that it is unaware of its own impending end.

Laughable—that is, deeply, irrevocably devoid of seriousness. As Eduard explains to his brother, how is it possible to "take seriously something so unserious" as a world stripped of reason? At a comedy show the only rule is burlesque, the only salvation a joke. Any serious, naive, or dignified person, one who never laughs, is inevitably the butt of farce and takes a drubbing. Only the character who understands beforehand what madness he is getting into, and who therefore knows that the only "morality" left to him is never to lose sight of this madness and not to try to fix or resist it, at the risk of being drubbed in turn, but just simply play the game and draw from it the maximum of amusement. He responds to the unseriousness of the world with the unseriousness of his existence.

One immediately thinks of Professor Avenarius in *Immortality*, a man with a penis decorated with a "horned devil's head," whose subversive acts against "Diabolum" sometimes take the form of the distribution of dunce caps to well-born donkeys, sometimes of a wild nocturnal ballet through the city streets spreading random disorder and causing damage. Avenarius, his friend the novelist remarks, acts "without method"; in every detail of his projects he is a pure anarchist; and above all, he is an anarchist with no illusions or program, who indulges in sabotage "only for [his] own, quite egotistical pleasure." "Jogging through the streets at night and puncturing tires is a great joy for the soul and excellent training for the body." With his "activism," but also with the at once good-natured and a bit enigmatic side of his character, Professor Avenarius (professor of what, by the way?), would feel at home in the small spa town of *Farewell Waltz*. There he would find a cheerful accomplice in Dr. Skreta, another expert manipulator who seems to have decided once and for all that the world is a joke and is therefore the exclusive province of buffoons. Nor would he be bored in the company of Bertlef, the émigré by birth who has returned to the homeland to die, yes, but to die a death whose approach seems boundlessly light and devoid of fuss—or "tralala"—as Céline put it.*

It might seem paradoxical to call Bertlef a "satanic" character, since he venerates icons and reads the Gospels. In the eyes of those who spend time with him—Klima, Skreta, Ruzena, even Jakub toward the end—he is rather a kind of saint. Yet, he is satanic as I use the term here, insofar as his gestures, his talk, his past (the scraps of it the novel provides are enough to put him under the sign of disillusion) make him, too, seem like a person who has withdrawn all belief from the world. But Bertlef, as we've seen, is also a master of the banquet, of hospitality, and of refinement; his disenchantment leads him neither to protest against the world nor to increase its disorder but to ignore or snub it, so to speak, making a protected, harmonious space in it for himself, a kind of enclave of gentleness and kindness. That second world neither replaces the first nor restores it, no more than Bertlef's vacation in the spa town, filled with conversation, encounters, and delicious meals, cures him of the illness that will soon carry him off, or than the feast he offers as if by magic to

*Cited by Kundera in "À bâtons rompus," *L'Atelier du roman* (May 1995) pp. 69–71.

Kamila's filmmaker friends brings back the old splendor of the "filthy café" in which it takes place. Just like this scene, the smiling light Bertlef lives amid is merely an "interlude," a diversion, which scoffs at the dying world that surrounds it still more forcefully but points up its death throes. This light is basically provisional, improbable, the light of what no longer exists; and Bertlef's strategy is that knowing this, he will act as if it still does.

Thus neither the affable, cheery face of the aesthete Bertlef nor the old-fashioned elegance of his ways make him a character so different from the saboteur Avenarius or the schemer Skreta. All three, in their ways, pit against the unseriousness of the world the same amused and nonbelieving attitude, made up of both casualness and a kind of mocking contempt; they respond to its unbearable lightness with the happy lightness of their capers and smiles; to God's absence they respond with the fullness of their own presence and the exercise of a freedom all the more cheerful for knowing itself to be unfettered. Their "satanism," in short, lies in their frivolity.

Although their attentiveness toward women is not presented as their main attribute, Avenarius, Skreta, and Bertlef all belong to that family of Kunderian characters whose satanic side is certainly the most pronounced: the "epic womanizers" (*The Unbearable Lightness of Being*). Not only have they broken off all commerce with history

and withdrawn all faith from everything but their immediate pleasure, not only do the singularity of their destiny
and the fate of the world leave them indifferent, but even
their exploits and conquests, while the sole focus of their
efforts, never completely—or all the way—receive the
seriousness that might keep them from toppling through
the trapdoor into laughter and meaninglessness. The
thing is that—unlike a romantic young lover—they know
the vanity and redundancies of love. Like Jan, they have
touched the border of repetition: Dr. Havel knows himself to be the comical double of a vanished original; the
narrator of "The Golden Apple of Eternal Desire"
knows that he is only "*playing*" at what Martin
"*lives*"—Martin who is only playing the stakeless game
of "*absolute pursuit*"; Rubens knows that no love is
unique and that "one and the same stream runs through
all men and women, a single, common subterranean river
sweeping erotic fantasies along." None of them, in short,
avoids the dilettante nature, "free . . . and revocable," of
their "boardings" and their conquests.

Awareness of the superficiality of the love chase,
however, is neither to disdain it nor to claim to set some
more "human," more "authentic," or more "subversive"
version of love to stand against it, as do Jaromil, Flajsman, and the other Kunderian virgins. It is, on the contrary, to accept, or at least to refuse to lose sight, of the

essential, irrevocable futility of having to live in a world devoid of seriousness, and trying to take on this futility in the most agreeable and elegant way, not only playing the game without forgetting that it is a game but playing it to perfection. That is why, in Kundera, the real Don Juan is never like a stallion, still less a rutting stallion. He is chasing after neither orgasm nor intoxication or domination of his partners. What spurs him on is the approach, the seduction, the boundlessly subtle mechanisms of arousal—that is, everything in the amorous exchange to do with the preliminary ballet, both physical and mental, in which the gestures, words, and thoughts primarily serve not to express some content (emotional or other) but to create a form. Thus the libertine, even when he is simulating love, is never lying. Because his terrain is not truth but pleasure. In this sense the great model of libertinism would be the transient relationship between Madame de T. and her young lover in *Slowness*. Each knows that nothing will come of this relationship, that in reality it is a relationship without substance or depth, which is neither binding nor significant and that will end when morning comes; nevertheless, far from despairing, far from trying to "transgress" the limits to which they know they are confined, they deploy all the delicacy, all the knowledge, and all the grace they are capable of to make of this choreography in which "everything is composed, confected, artificial," in which "nothing is straightforward," a moment of unforgettable richness.

An episode of pure pleasure and bliss. The notion of "episode," which I discussed in the preceding chapter, concerns not only the techniques of novelistic composition. It is also—like everything that pertains to the novel's aesthetic—an ethical category. It could be defined as the libertine or satanic version—that is, the degraded, profane, ironic version—of the idea of *destiny*; or better, as what remains of that idea once the border is crossed beyond which values collapse while "the devil of laughter" triumphs. In the same way as tragedy, history, or truth and justice, destiny does in fact assume a stable, orderly universe, or at least the possibility of such a universe. As soon as this possibility vanishes, as soon as the metaphysical, moral, and historical signposts that gave it continuity and meaning fall, as soon as the mind knows, as Kundera's Jacques teaches the Innkeeper, that "nothing on earth is certain, and [that] the meaning of things changes as the wind blows," existence immediately loses any characteristic of necessity, any semblance of direction and progress, so that the destiny model can absolutely no longer fit. What happens to existence then is what happens to the novel when it no longer wants to "be like a bicycle race" and abandons linear composition based on a logical chain of actions: its unity comes apart, its "dramatic tension" drops, its unfolding slows, to the point when its every moment ceases to be a "step leading to the final resolution," and finds its value and meaning only in itself. There is no longer an overall plan, no longer a scenario. Deprived of the unifying perspective of destiny, what remains of life becomes an assemblage of detached sequences, lacking both cause and effect—that is, lacking controllable cause and foreseeable effect, each having its beginning and end in itself and each possessing its own temporality, color, and logic: simply episodes. Admittedly a link might exist between the episodes—common theme(s), recurrences, "existential code"—and their arrangement, like that of the novel in the form of variations, might create a recognizable overall design; but the link and arrangement are not the sort that govern the dramatic progess of an adventure or a quest; they do not order the episodes of existence relative to each other, making one the condition or result of another; they preserve to each its full autonomy, its mystery, and its fragile beauty.

Episode, the libertine morality of episode, in other words, is life freed from destiny—from destiny's unswerving route—and becomes like a random walk on mountain paths, where every stretch, every crossing, is loved for itself because it has its own value and meaning. Such, par excellence in Part Six of *Immortality*, is the affair of Agnès and Rubens, who "know only the barest minimum about each other, and they are almost proud of having concealed their lives in the shadows so that their meetings will be lit up all the more brightly, divorced from time and circumstance." He becomes attached to her because in his eyes she is "a real princess of episode," appearing in his life at the moment when "the hands on the dial had brought his sexual life full circle" and "women were of no importance to him." As for her, not only does this affair unfold on the margins of her married and family life but there she is also freed of her name (Rubens simply calls her the "lute player"), of her face (which she conceals behind her gestures), even of her very soul (we never enter it), finally separated from her own destiny.

Another inhabitant of episode: the man in his forties of *Life Is Elsewhere*. He has no name either, and all we know of his biography is that it has driven him to pull away and absent himself from the world where it took place, and end up "outside the drama of his own life . . . his back turned on History and its dramatic performances, his back turned on his own destiny, he himself entirely preoccupied with himself, with his private, responsibility-free amusements and his books." No matter that he is still in his own country; he lives there like an émigré, like a person who has crossed the border and who, from his new "observatory," concerned only to protect "the idyll of his nondestiny," is looking from afar at the country with which he has broken.

The Exile

The man in his forties is the bridge between a first mode of the Kunderian universe—the one that I've called "satanic," embodied in exemplary fashion by the figure of the libertine—and another somewhat different mode that is to the first what the serious is to the light, adagio to allegro, dusk to broad daylight. This second mode, less often noticed although it is present in every part of the novelist's oeuvre, can be called the exile mode.

To understand its function and meaning, let's again ask this question: How do you go on living when you have crossed the border and ceased to believe in the world's seriousness? Or in Agnès's actual terms:

> How to live in a world with which you disagree?
> How to live with people when you share neither their
> suffering nor their joys? When you know that you
> don't belong among them?

A first possibility, some of whose consequences we have just seen, consists of remaining in the world

despite everything but, like an internal exile, respond-
ing to its enticements with the "lucid, unillusioned eye"
of the nonbeliever, to its fancy displays with irony, to its
irrepressible need for plenitude with the intoxication of
laughter and games—that is to say, never ceasing to
consider the world what it denies being: an enormous
joke. This attitude is at the root of a fundamental
dimension of Kundera's oeuvre and of his practice of
the novel as profanation, demystification, as the critical, even sarcastic, denuding, the unending devastation,
of the illusions and ravages that come from serious
mindedness. Everything falls before that attitude—lyricism, revolutionary faith, media optimism, the desire
for innocence, the need for brotherhood and certainty
and justice. These are snares, all of them, screens that
the prose takes pleasure in taking apart one by one,
piece by piece, to keep alive the consciousness that
gave it birth—that of its own fall in a universe that the
absence of God has turned into what the author of
Testaments Betrayed calls a "carnival of relativity" in
which everyone, without exception, dupes himself and
is duped by others, beginning with the one who doesn't
know it. But there is still another possible way, for
someone who has crossed the border, to confront the
world: to leave for good and never return. To cut all
bonds, even bonds of subversion or disgust, and to set-

tle permanently somewhere remote, where the world no longer reaches him.

That already was, in a certain way, the choice of the man in his forties; that is, the necessity in which he had been placed by his political disgrace. Because often, as we've already seen with regard to the figure of the *banished* person, the one who experiences banishment finds through his very experience an exile that liberates. Doomed to exclusion or marginality, "thrown off [his] life's path," he discovers a paradoxical happiness right at the core of that exclusion, as if being driven from the world freed him from it and as if his removal caused him to enter a homeland long lost and finally recovered. The best example is that of Ludvik during his relegation to Ostrava, when he is touched by Lucie's slowness and *"ordinariness"*:

> I was convinced that far from the wheel of History there was no life, only vegetation, boredom, exile, Siberia. And suddenly (after six months of Siberia) I'd found a new and unexpected opportunity for life: I saw spread before me, hidden beneath History's soaring wings, a forgotten meadow of everyday life, where a poor, pitiful, but lovable woman was waiting for me—Lucie.
>
> What did Lucie know of the great wings of History? When could she have heard their sound? She knew nothing of History, she lived *beneath* it; it held

no attraction for her, it was alien to her; she knew nothing of the *great* and *contemporary* concerns; she lived for her *small* and *eternal* concerns. And suddenly I'd been liberated.

But Ludvik is still too young for such a liberation. As soon as his sentence has been served, he falls back into the desire not to "shirk [his] fate" and forgets about the "*gray paradise*" Lucie offered him. Only at the end, when the joke of his entire adventure will dawn on him, does he go back to it by joining Jaroslav's outdated little folk orchestra, "a desert island" in the midst of a rowdy crowd and a "devastated world."

In *The Book of Laughter and Forgetting*, Tamina and her husband have a similar experience after they are forced out of their homeland—the experience of exile as rupture and respite both, loss and safety at the same time.

> On the first morning after their flight, when they awoke in a small hotel in an alpine village and realized that they were alone, cut off from the world where all of their lives had been spent, she experienced a feeling of liberation and relief. They were in the mountains, marvelously alone. Around them unbelievable silence reigned. Tamina welcomed that silence as an unexpected gift.

Where did this feeling of liberation and relief come from, as if, instead of depriving them of their home, emigration had finally brought them to it? It came from solitude and silence, Tamina thought. Meaning: from the move away from their homeland, away from all of the homeland within them, to which from now on they were no longer bound by any contract or affection; that is to say, from their own move across the border beyond which no thing or person can any longer know or betray them, where they belong to nothing, where history and destiny fall silent and leave them in peace.

This vision of exile runs through Kundera's entire oeuvre, where the theme acts as a leitmotiv, a constant fascination. Eduard's brother, in *Laughable Loves*, or Bob's owners, in *Farewell Waltz*, are of the same family as the man in his forties. Sabina, in *The Unbearable Lightness of Being*, seeks only "betrayal" and estrangement; her existence is an endless emigration. Chantal, the heroine of *Identity*, is also an émigré in a way: her age, the death of her child, and above all her love for Jean-Marc (experienced as "a transgression of the unwritten laws of the human community") have released her from all obligations and quests.

> She relished the utter absence of adventures. Adventure: a means of embracing the world. She no longer wanted to embrace the world.

The theme reappears, and still more powerfully, in *Ignorance*, which recounts the return of two émigrés, Irena and Josef, to their birthplace, Bohemia, after twenty years abroad. It is therefore a novel of the end of exile, of the return home. But how to begin again to live in a world you have fled? The homeland they come back to seems to them unrecognizable, hostile, emptied of substance and sincerity. The regime has changed, of course, but not the people, their errors, and their lies; it is the same old existence, the same comedy, the more ridiculous now for thinking itself innocent and free. So after a few days, though he loves his country, Josef starts to have this paradoxical feeling: nostalgia for exile. He realizes that his homeland can no longer be his homeland and that from now on he has only one dwelling place, and it is his place of exile, far from here, far from the fighting and the settling of accounts, where awaiting him are "two easy chairs turned to face each other, the lamp and the flower bowl on the window ledge, and the slender fir tree his wife planted in front of the house, a fir tree that looks like an arm she'd raised from afar to show him the way back home." *Ignorance*, in other words, isn't so much a novel about return as about its impossibility.

But the most detailed image of exile existence, the

one that pushes its description furthest and serves as a
kind of background for all the others, is of course Part
Seven of *The Unbearable Lightness of Being*, in which
Tomas and Tereza, "in a place that led nowhere" and
having reached the end of their problems with themselves
and with their destiny, having "cut their life in two like a
ribbon," leave Prague and go off to bury themselves far
from everything, sheltered from everything, with no concern but their love, their daily bread, and the happiness of
the dying Karenin. These pages are among the most gripping in Kundera's oeuvre because they make a lengthy
experience, we might say, of what elsewhere most often
remains a fleeting moment of insight, dream, or appeal.
The setting: an isolated, archaic village, where nature
seems free of man's power; the characters' situation:
Tomas a truck driver, Tereza a cowherd, both socially
diminished, poor, and without a "mission" or plan; their
solitude; the time they live in: shapeless, with no trajectory, become pure routine, pure repetition, infinite slowness: we are here in the absolute of exile. While the
"Grand March" of history continues elsewhere, around
Tomas and Tereza the world has completely vanished,
along with its turbulences, mirages, and desires; what
remains is only silence and repose. Along with Tereza's
feeling of an "odd happiness" and an "odd sadness":

"The sadness was form, the happiness content. Happiness filled the space of sadness."

If Tomas and Tereza's withdrawal—like Josef's and that of the other figures I've just mentioned—draws on aspects of the *idyll*—that is to say, of a "condition of the world before the first conflict; or beyond conflicts; or with conflicts that are only misunderstandings, thus false conflicts" (*The Art of the Novel*), still a particular feature of this idyll is that it is based neither on unawareness of conflicts nor on their resolution (real or supposed), but on capitulation. The conflicts are not denied, they are abandoned; and it is neither his innocence nor his strength that opens the doors of this idyll to the exiled person; it is only his refusal to fight, the exhaustion of all his innocence and strength. The idyll is granted him not as a victory, not as the return to a primordial paradise lost, and still less as the entry into a future utopia won by a hard-fought struggle, but rather as a cessation, a "last station" completely under the sign of forgetting, resignation, and fatigue, which will become one of the essential themes of *Immortality*:

> A weary man looks out of the window, sees the tops of trees, and silently recites their names: chestnut, poplar, maple. And those names are as beautiful as being itself. The poplar is tall and looks like an ath-

lete raising his arm to the sky. Or it looks like a flame that has soared into the air and petrified. Poplar, oh poplar.

"Fatigue: a silent bridge leading from the shore of life to the shore of death." One might also say about exile that it is life lived next to death: Tomas and Tereza know that Karenin will soon die, and we know, because it has already been announced, that their own death is imminent, that they are already in its shadow. Likewise, the foreign home Josef longs for is just an isolated house inhabited by the memory of his deceased wife. Tamina, too, is widowed, and focused exclusively on her ever-more-distant past. As for Chantal, beside the grave of her child she is able to say: "By your death you deprived me of the pleasure of being with you, but at the same time you set me free. Free in my confrontation with the world I don't like. And the reason I can allow myself to dislike it is that you're no longer here." Like the dead, the exiled person is no longer among the living, and that is probably the source of his "odd sadness" and "odd happiness."

This proximity to death is moreover what gives the idyll of exile its negative nature and makes it the exact opposite of "kitsch": mortality is not denied in it, but, on the contrary, fully accepted, and with it imperfection, transience, and corruption. It is, therefore, a prosaic, unillusioned idyll, whose walls are built of that "categorical disagreement," that absolute disavowal which frees the exile both from the world and from his destiny.*

One of the attributes—and great audacities—of Kundera's oeuvre is this recurrent central place occupied by the theme—and the ethic—of exile, either as representation or aspiration. For it isn't self-evident that the novel, which has always been defined primarily as a hero's adventure, and whose favored material is action, quest, conflict, could admit so much of immobility and abandon without destroying itself. How can the novel, as "an investigation of human life in the trap the world has become," as Kundera puts it in *The Unbearable Lightness of Being*, also investigate human life when it has freed itself of that trap and left the world? Isn't exile, in a way, located beyond its aesthetic and ontological borders?

As for the aesthetic, we've seen that one of the basic ambitions of Kundera's oeuvre is precisely to shift the traditional borders of the novel so as to free it from the exclusive domination of action and fighting. The model of the path-novel, the rehabilitation of episode, the "continuous and changing" form of variations, the art of

---

*On the subject of idyll figures in Kundera, see my article "Mortalité d'Agnès," *L'Infini* 35 (Fall 1991), reprinted as a postface to the Folio edition of *L'Immortalité*.

ellipsis and of the brief chapter are just so many ways of inventing another type of novel in which what I call the exile mode—devaluation of adventure, interrupted action, temporality based on slowness and repetition, a thematic of rupture and separation—appears not as an interlude or a foreign body but rather constitutes the essence, the ground on which the whole organization and the whole meaning of the oeuvre rest. This means—from the ontological point of view—that in the Kunderian novel exile existence will be not so much its material as its source; not so much the thing it investigates as its very method of investigation. His privileged observatory, to return to the image in Part Six of *Life Is Elsewhere*. Because to see the world as a trap requires, in a manner of speaking, to have cut loose from it. Now that God has withdrawn and his place is forever vacant, now that any viewpoint from above has become impracticable, isn't the only modern way to free oneself of fondness for the world to leave it, to fall out of it, below it, beside it into the alien and negative places of exile?

The exiled person; the libertine. The creature of departure and solitude; the creature of laughter and play. Between these two figures, of course, there is no opposition. Moreover, both often happen to be embodied in the same character: in the man in his forties and in Rubens—

where they practically coincide—and, above all, in Tomas, where they could not succeed or replace each other as they do if they weren't actually each other's double or reverse side. Sabina understands that well, in fact, when, after learning of Tomas's death, she thinks of him "as if he were one of her paintings: Don Juan in the foreground, a specious stage-set by a naive painter, and through a crack in the set—Tristan." And Tereza, too, understands him, continuing almost to the end to see behind her Tristan the ghost of Don Juan. Libertinism and exile, laughter and escape, far from creating contradictory universes, are merely two ways of placing oneself in relation to the same border, two ways of inhabiting the same world become like a "valueless chaos" (*Identity*). The exile has been a libertine; the libertine will be an exile. Neither in the one case nor the other can they grant the world the credit and the seriousness it claims.

Epilogue

"When you cross the border," thinks Jan, "laughter fatefully rings out. But what if you go still farther, go *beyond* laughter?" We might answer him: Beyond laughter there lies exile. But what lies beyond exile?

Let's come back one last time to Agnès in repose.

Her happiness initially comes from this taste of a perfect moment of solitude and tranquillity in the midst of a landscape she loves. She who suffers from living in an era from which charterhouses have vanished and in which there is no longer "a place secluded from people and the world" briefly experiences the consolation of exile, which for her is also a return to her only home-land: the mountain path where her dead father smiles and calls to her. But it is not only the fact of being cut off from people and the world that makes Agnès happy, or the fact of escaping "the dirt of the self." More deeply, it is that for a few hours she can finally be free from the obligation of "living":

> The secondary road she drove onto from the highway was quiet, and distant stars, infinitely distant stars, shone over it. Agnès drove on and thought:
>
> Living, there is no happiness in that. Living: carrying one's hurting self through the world.
>
> But being, being is happiness. Being: becoming a fountain, a fountain on which the universe falls like warm rain.

Her happiness, in other words, is not only knowing herself to be alone, free, exiled from everyone, but also being, for a moment, as if she no longer existed, as if everything of herself had withdrawn, faded out, been abolished, and as if by this obliteration there might finally shine forth "that primordial being, which manifested itself in the voice of fleeting time and the blue of the sky."

Imagination here reaches an ultimate point: conceiving own disappearance. This dream or vision of a "primordial" world runs just beneath the surface of all of Kundera's oeuvre. Perfectly silent, at peace, "freed of aggressive and burdensome . . . human subjectivity," (*Testaments Betrayed*) it would be a world "finally . . . free . . . from mankind's clutches," (*Farewell Waltz*), a world outside which man, with all the jumble of his history, of his feelings and his destiny, would have taken his final *sidestep*.

Then the peace promised to Agnès by the Goethe poem her father used to recite to her would finally be established:

> *Über allen Gipfeln*
> *Ist Ruh,*
> *In allen Wipfeln*
> *Spürest du*
> *Kaum einen Hauch;*
> *Die Vögelein schweigen im Walde.*
> *Warte nur, balde*
> *Ruhest du auch.*

(On all hilltops
There is peace,
In all treetops
You will hear
Hardly a breath.
Birds in the woods are silent.
Just wait, soon
You too will rest.)

All being would become a "fountain on which the universe falls like warm rain," dogs and other animals would be at home, nature would extend everywhere, there would be no more world, no more laughter or love, no more paths or exile. And no more novel.

Bibliography

BY MILAN KUNDERA

All the quotations herein from Kundera's works are from their most recent English-language translations.

Novels

The Joke: translated from the Czech by David Hamblyn and Oliver Stallybrass, Coward-McCann, Inc., 1969; retranslated from the Czech by Michael Henry Heim, Harper & Row, Publishers, 1982; revised by the author and Aaron Asher, HarperCollins Publishers, 1992.

Laughable Loves: translated from the Czech by Suzanne Rappaport, Alfred A. Knopf, Inc., 1974; revised by the author and Aaron Asher, HarperCollins Publishers, 1999.

Life Is Elsewhere: translated from the Czech by Peter Kussi, Alfred A. Knopf, Inc., 1974; retranslated from the French by Aaron Asher, HarperCollins Publishers, 2000.

Farewell Waltz: translated from the Czech under the title *The Farewell Party* by Peter Kussi, Alfred A. Knopf, Inc., 1976; retranslated from the French by Aaron Asher, HarperCollins Publishers, 1998.

The Book of Laughter and Forgetting: translated from the Czech by Michael Henry Heim, Alfred A. Knopf, Inc., 1980; retranslated from the French by Aaron Asher, HarperCollins Publishers, 1996.

The Unbearable Lightness of Being: translated from the Czech by Michael Henry Heim, Harper & Row, Publishers, 1984; HarperCollins Publishers, 1999.

Immortality: translated from the Czech by Peter Kussi, Grove Press, 1991; HarperCollins Publishers, 1992.

Slowness: translated from the French by Linda Asher, HarperCollins Publishers, 1995.

Identity: translated from the French by Linda Asher, HarperCollins Publishers, 1997.

Ignorance: translated from the French by Linda Asher, HarperCollins Publishers, 2002.

Play

Jacques and His Master: An Homage to Diderot in Three Acts: translated from the French by Michael Henry Heim, Harper & Row, Publishers, 1985.

Essays

The Art of the Novel: translated from the French by Linda Asher, Grove Press, 1988; HarperCollins Publishers, 2000.

Testaments Betrayed: translated from the French by Linda Asher, HarperCollins Publishers, 1995, 2001.

CRITICISM

Books

Aji, Aron, ed. *Milan Kundera and the Art of Fiction: Critical Essays*. New York: Garland Publishing, 1992.

Banerjee, Maria Němcová. *Terminal Paradox: The Novels of Milan Kundera*. New York: Grove Press, 1992.

Misurella, Fred. *Understanding Milan Kundera: Public Events, Private Affairs*. Columbia: University of South Carolina Press, 1993.

Chvatik, Kvetoslav. *Le Monde romanesque de Milan Kundera*, translated from the German by Bernard

Lortholary, with ten hitherto unpublished texts by Milan Kundera. Paris: Gallimard, 1995.

Le Grand, Eva. *Kundera ou la Mémoire du désir*, preface by Guy Scarpetta. Paris and Montreal: L'Harmattan and XYZ, 1995.

Scarpetta, Guy. *L'Age d'or du roman*. Paris: Grasset, 1996.

Maixent, Jocelyn. *Le XVIIIe siècle de Milan Kundera, ou Diderot investi par le roman contemporain*. Paris: Presses universitaires de France, 1998.

Nishinaga, Yoshinari. *Milan Kundera's Philosophy of the Novel*. Tokyo: Heibonsha Sensho, 1998 (in Japanese).

Boisen, Jørn. *Milan Kundera: En Introduktion*. Copenhagen: Gyldendal, 2001.

Periodicals

Liberté 121. January–February 1979.

Salmagundi 73. Winter 1987.

The Review of Contemporary Fiction IX–2. Summer 1989.

Dix-neuf vingt 1. March 1996.

Riga 20, Milan, 2002.